Prophecy:
What Could Be

Rev. Brannon M. Drees

Contents

To Stephanie and Alex:
Sorry I didn't see you much while you were growing up,
I was out doing "research"
Also dedicated to Delana and Gabriella,
May you find Peace, Love, and Happiness

Preface

"Ask and it will be given to you; seek and you will find; knock and the door will be opened to you." – **Jesus 0-34**[1]

" . . . you must worship Christ as Lord of your life. And if someone asks about your Christian hope, always be ready to explain it." – **Saint Peter 1 BC - 67 AD**[2]

"I am not afraid . . . I was born to do this." – **Joan of Arc 1412-1431**[3]

"You are not only responsible for what you say, but also for what you do not say" – **Martin Luther 1483-1546**[4]

THIS BOOK IS a 100 page attempt to lay out a plan to save the planet and the people on it within 7 generations. The prophecy I am referring to is the observation that, if we continue to do what we are doing, we and future generations are all going to regret it. I guess

---

[1] *Matthew 7:7 ""Ask and it will be given to you; seek and you will find; knock and the door will be opened to you."* (n.d.). retrieved from http://bible.ccl/matthew/7.7.htm

[2] *Bible - New Living Translation - 1Peter3:15.* (n.d.) Retrieved from http://bible.cc/1_peter/3-15.htm

[3] *Joan of Arc quotes.*(n.d.). Retrieved from http://en.thinkexist.com/quotes/Joan_of_Arc

[4] *Martin Luther quotes.* (n.d.). Retrieved from http://en.thinkexist.com/quotes/martin_luther/

anyone and everyone can see that coming. I also show what could be, if alternatively, we follow a different path for seven generations. The environment could be saved, and every person would have their basic needs met, and be happy, or at least content. The ideas I propose should be universally acceptable, because they are in everyone's best interests.

Many civilizations, empires, religions, and philosophies have attempted to create a perfect society or "utopia." About 447 years before Christ was born, the Greeks were building the Parthenon, and many other architectural wonders like the Acropolis. I had a chance to see many of them while I was there. I also saw the "mount" from Saint John's "Sermon on the Mount." The Greeks had and still have one of the greatest civilizations of all time.

Next, the road I was on led to Rome, which was certainly the greatest civilization of its time and is quite possibly the greatest civilization of all time. Like me, the Pope was traveling, so I did not get to see him, but I did get to see Saint Peter's Basilica and the Sistine Chapel. I took a self guided tour that ended with me looking directly up and seeing God. That was one of the most moving experiences in my life. Looking back with 20/20 hindsight, maybe that was a self-guided tour, within a self-guided tour that was my life, whereas now I'm on a mission to save as many children as I can.

I have been to 45 of the United States and over 40 nations. I have spent over 4 years outside of the US in Latin America, Europe, and Asia, studying other civilizations, formerly great empires, as well as, different religions and philosophies among other things. My goal is to visit Africa, Australia, and Antarctica, so I will be one of a few people that have been to every continent.

When I traveled in Europe, I got to see places like England, Ireland, Northern Ireland, Scotland, France, Belgium, The Netherlands, Germany, Austria, Switzerland, The former Czechoslovakia, The former Yugoslavia, Turkey, Greece, Italy, Vatican City, Monte Carlo, Spain, and Portugal. I've also seen parts of Asia including Japan, South Korea, and China. I've seen most of the cities in the Americas as well.

I got to see Churchill's War Room, and I toured the White House, from which, Roosevelt commanded the US Military in WWII. I'm one of the few people in the world that has been to London, Washington D.C., Berlin and Tokyo. I studied World War II extensively. Humans who don't learn from history, are doomed to repeat it. I visited both Dachau near Munich and the Holocaust Museum in Washington D.C. and was moved to tears. All it takes for evil to succeed is for good people to do nothing.

Every year 6 million children die whose deaths were preventable. This is an annual holocaust, a never ending genocide.

When I was living in and around the rainforest for 90 days, I not only saw how billions of poor people on earth live, I lived as they live. Life is not easy for most of the people on earth. They have no conveniences, they live in unsanitary conditions where they have little if any food. They may have too little if any drinkable water, and no water for irrigation. They have no health, dental, and vision care, and they usually have inadequate shelter. They rarely have any formal education. There is rarely any opportunity, and not a lot of hope.

On the other end of the spectrum, Seoul is called the "miracle on the Han," because it went from being rubble in 1953, to being the world's largest metropolis by 2003. The city is not perfect, but it is a testament to what people with nothing can do in 50 years time. There is an open-air stadium right in the heart of Seoul, it is surrounded by skyscrapers. It is very near the 600 year old Namdaemun "Great South Gate". I was there to celebrate Buddha's 2544 birthday. Everyone had a little candle lit lantern. It was so peaceful, words can not describe it.

I once took a course where we talked about Capitalism qualified by morality. It seems like many people are getting fed up with the immoral, unethical, soulless, corporations exploiting and enslaving people for profit and over charging the end consumer on top of it. The government is just as guilty of overcharging the consumer. Not too many taxpayers feel like they get their money's worth. I prefer and promote nonprofits over for-profit companies and government agencies. I have seen first hand what Unicef does, and that is what needs to be done, and they know how to do it better than anyone. Especially when it comes to supplying billions of people with water, food, healthcare, housing, and education.

Once, while I was in London, I drank a glass of French wine older than me, in a pub older than the United States, that had been frequented by Karl Marx while he was writing in London. There is now over a billion Marxists, Communists, Socialists, and others who do not like Capitalism and have no need for religion. I have peeked behind Russia's Iron Curtain (East Berlin). I have also been to China and two other communist/socialist nations (Venezuela and Bolivia). Communism and socialism are the fastest growing movements in human history. Russia has 21.5 million troops, China 4.6 mil., North Korea 9.5 mil., Vietnam 5.5 mil.

The world spends around 1.5 trillion on military spending, the US who is 14 trillion in debt spends about 687 billion on its military annually.

Comparatively, they spend only about 23 billion on foreign aid. The world is not going to be saved in 4 or 8 years, especially not by the US taxpayers, it is going to take a multigenerational resolution and a concerted, coordinated effort on behalf of millions of people with resources to help the billions of people in extreme and absolute poverty.

There will be the inevitable wars, revolutions, diseases, and famines. There will be natural disasters in places like Haiti where they got hit by hurricanes and earthquakes, and little kids were eating mud cakes because there was not any food. The U.N. does all it can, feeding millions with their World Food Programme. The WHO (World Health Organization) is doing all they can attending to sick children. Others such as Unicef are doing everything within their power as well. Great strides are being made, but this is a marathon and humanity is no where near the finish line.

I even tried to do my part. My ill fated attempt at noblesse oblige was sponsoring girls in Bolivia, El Salvador, and almost a girl in Haiti, three of the poorest nations in the Western Hemisphere. I used to like writing them, and receiving their letters, and sending them little care packages with stuff like little mini shampoo bottles. Not long after I started sponsoring, Haiti got rocked by the earthquake that claimed 316,000 lives, injured another 300,000, and left another 1 million homeless. The girl I would have sponsored most likely did not make it. A building could have collapsed on her, and they would have had no machines to dig her out, and no way to get water to her, so she would have died of dehydration, trapped under the concrete.

This next decade could be the tipping point not just for the environment, but for humanity as well. We should make sure every child has water, food, healthcare, shelter, education, opportunity, hope, and love. In addition to that, it would be in human's best interests not to do any more damage to the environment than they have already done. On the contrary, humans should start repairing the damage they have done or the planet won't be habitable by anyone.

I am not a writer or a scientist, so please forgive my many mistakes. I do not expect to win a Pulitzer prize, but maybe this book will inspire a future Pulitzer or Nobel Prize winner. That would be worth more to me than money. I would like to hear your comments and any constructive criticism you may have, so I can make the next edition better. Please email me at *prophecy.what.could.be@gmail.com.*

Introduction

"Ballots are the rightful and peaceful successors to bullets." – **Abraham Lincoln**[5] **1809-1865**

"Be the change you want to see in the world." – **Gandhi**[6] **1869-1948**

"A man may die, nations may rise and fall, but an idea lives on." – **John F. Kennedy**[7] **1917-1963 (November 22nd)**

"Almost always, the creative dedicated minority has made the world better." – **MLK, Jr.**[8] **1929-1968 (April 4th)**

"There are those who look at things the way they are, and ask why . . . I dream of things that never were, and ask why not?" – **Robert F. Kennedy**[9] **1925-1968 (June 6th)**

5   http://www.brainyquote.com/quotes/quotes/a/abrahamlin139326.html
6   http://thinkexist.com/quotation/be_the_change_you_want_to_see_in_the_world/148490.html
7   http://thinkexist.com/quotation/a_man_may_die-nations_may_rise_and_fall-but_an/148060.html
8   http://thinkexist.com/quotation/almost_always-the_creative_dedicated_minority_has/216342.html
9   http://www.brainyquote.com/quotes/quotes/r/robertkenn121273.html

"Imagine all the people living life in peace . . . and the world could live as one." – **John Lennon**[10] **1940-1980**

"How long shall they kill our prophets, while we stand aside and look?" – **Bob Marley**[11] **1945-1981**

THE FOLLOWING IS one possible course of action for the years 2015-2150. It may seem improbable, or even impossible . . .

The year 2015: Generation 1 could be born in the United States to parents who have taken parenting classes and are licensed to parent. These parents could also establish a trust fund for each child. Most parents would choose to have only one or two children. Parents could continue to take parenting classes and meet a parenting standard until the child is 18. At age 4, all children in the US could start using the Fast Track Program which could track their progress until they were 18. At age 13, Generation 1 could become the first group of children to attend the National Academies. These could be new "super schools" built in the US, with every feature, every elective and extracurricular activity, every amenity imaginable. Students would live on-site all year and study a wide range of subjects. Students could develop an admiration for their nation, and a sense of national pride and devotion. After graduating the National Academy at 18, Generation 1 could go on to do required National Service in either a branch of the Military, the Peace Corps, Americorps/Vista, or some type of missionary work. Upon completion of their National Service, based on their performance, they could be assigned a level and offered a career that is right for them. They could easily advance to higher levels with additional education and training. Generation 1 could then be paired off with their perfect mate using the Matchmaker Program. They could get married, go on a honeymoon, and when they get back, they could start taking parenting classes. Once they have completed all of the parenting classes and passed their parenting exam, they could be ready to breed Generation 2. The family could then move into some form of "cookie cutter" housing, such as a 3 bedroom 2 bathroom condominium in a chain of cookie cutter condos that have all of the amenities a young family would want. One or both

---

[10] http://www.lyrics007.com/John%20Lennon%20Lyrics/Imagine%20Lyrics.htm

[11] http://www.lyricsera.com/556457-lyric-Bob+Marley-Redemption.html

parents could work until their one or two children have been sent to the National Academy. Once the students graduate the Academy and go on to do their National Service, the parents may choose to retire early to one of thousands of new cookie cutter retirement villas in exotic locations all over the US, and around the world. Each Generation could become successively more advanced than the previous one was at their age. They could repeat this process, and by about Generation 4, all of the people in the nation could have graduated from an Academy, and done their National Service. They could have all worked until they were in their 40's or 50's, and could have all retired to the new cookie cutter retirement villas.

Each Generation could be taught the concept of *noblesse oblige,* which should instill in them a desire to help the less fortunate in the US, and the world, when and where they can. They could be trained exceptionally well and given the tools they need to repair the world within 7 generations. Generation 1 (born about 2015-2035) could work on making sure every woman has a birth control implant effective for up to 3 years. Generation 1 could also make sure that everyone in the world who decides to have a child gets some parenting classes, and obtains some sort of parenting license. Generation 2 (2035-2055) could be responsible for building thousands of water desalination plants all over the world and laying a network of pipelines that bring water to every inch of the earth. There could be an abundance of water for drinking, bathing, cleaning, and, of course, irrigation which uses 70% of the world's water. This could not only provide every world citizen with an abundance of free water, it could be able to increase the amount of arable land used for agricultural purposes. There could also be an abundance of water for irrigation meaning bigger agricultural yields than ever before. This could significantly increase the amount of food the planet is producing, making it much easier for Generation 3 (2055-2075) whose top priority could be to make sure every person, especially children, gets enough to eat. With an abundance of food being produced, it could just be a matter of processing, packaging and shipping the food to its final destination. Logistics could be simplified with high-speed trains, semi's running on biodiesel, and other new inventions that could make it easier and cheaper and more eco-friendly to get products and people to more places faster and safer than ever before. Generation 4 (2075-2095) could be in charge of making sure that every child has adequate health care available at low or no cost to their parents. They can also set up a chain of international clinics that could provide extremely inexpensive and oftentimes free services to everyone, everywhere in the world. Generation 5 (2095-2115) could be responsible for making sure every world citizen has adequate housing. From cookie cutter shelters to more prestigious cookie cutter condominiums, everyone, everywhere could have a decent place to call home. Generation 6 (2115-2135) could make sure that every child receives not only an education, but that they learn the same core curriculum as every other child in the world. This would ensure that all the world's children could have much more in common making it easier for them to assimilate as adults, and making it easier for international law makers to achieve a consensus. Generation 7 (2135-2155) can work on repairing any and all damage done to the environment including saving all wildlife. They could also work on creating enough economic opportunity for everyone without doing harm to anyone or to the environment.

If humans continue to make the same mistakes over and over again, by the year 2150, if there is even anyone left, it could be an overcrowded, polluted planet with over 10 billion people in poverty, experiencing wars, plagues, famines, and natural disasters they are not prepared for.

Conversely, humans could be living in a utopian world they and their ancestors have created for themselves, and their future generations to inherit.

In the coming chapters, we will see how we could one day get water, food, healthcare, shelter, education, and economic opportunity to every child born in the US and eventually every child in the world. Albert Einstein said, "When the solution is easy, God is answering"[12]

---

[12]   http://hubpages.com/hub/Science-and-Religion-Are-they-enemies-or-friends

1

The Child is the Father of the Man[13]

MANY CHILDREN IN the US are not being raised correctly. Statistically speaking, in the future, many of them will become adults who do not raise their children correctly. If this growing cycle of dysfunction continues, it could be catastrophic to the US.

The solutions could be as simple as birth control implants that last for 3 years, parenting classes, parenting licenses and a parenting standard. These measures could break this cycle of dysfunction and help repair the nation.

Many mothers are having children out of wedlock. Many of these pregnancies are unplanned. There can not be a law requiring young women and women to take birth control, nor can their be a law requiring them to be married and have a parenting license, but there can be incentives if they choose to wait until they are mentally, physically, and financially prepared to have a child and if they get married and stay married. Over 25 % of children are being raised in single parent households. This can not bode well for the nation. Childbearing has to be taken more seriously. Every mother, single or married, should be

---

[13]   http://www.bartleby.com/145/ww194.html

mentally, physically, and financially prepared to raise children. Future mothers could wait to have children until they are married. They could be encouraged to get married and stay married as well as take parenting classes, get a parenting license, and meet a parenting standard. There could be incentives for them if they do so.

Child abuse is far to common and can be extreme. Bullying incidents are much too frequent and can be severe. The high number of teen runaways, teen homelessness, and teen suicides are signs that children are sometimes not being raised in positive environments. Many youth are joining gangs as a solution to their problems. There are a growing number of crimes, including violent crimes, being committed by young adults. There are record numbers of young adults in juvenile detention centers and some are even tried as adults in some cases. A large number of teens use and abuse alcohol and drugs with many ending up in rehab centers. In some areas more kids quit school than finish. Then there is the alarming number of teen pregnancies. All of this leads to more broken homes and dysfunctional "families." The only things the children of these "parents' and "families" will "inherit" are their mental, physical, and financial problems. It would take a library of books to tell all of the stories individually, so here are some statistics.

Child Abuse in the United States

"Children are suffering from a hidden epidemic of child abuse. Over 3 million reports of child abuse are made every year in the United States; however, those reports can include multiple children being abused in a single report making the number of children being abused far more than 3 million. In 2007, approximately 5.8 million children were involved in an estimated 3.2 million child abuse reports and allegations.

General Statistics

- **A report of child abuse is made every ten seconds.**
- Almost **five children die every day** as a result of child abuse. More than three out of four are under the age of 4.
- It is estimated that between 60-85% of child fatalities due to maltreatment are **not recorded as such on death certificates.**

- 90% of child sexual abuse victims know the perpetrator in some way; 68% are abused by family members.
- Child abuse occurs at every socioeconomic level, across ethnic and cultural lines, within all religions and at all levels of education.
- 31% percent of women in prison in the United States were abused as children.
- Over **60% of people in drug rehabilitation centers report being abused or neglected** as a child.
- About 30% of abused and neglected children **could later abuse their own children,** continuing the horrible cycle of abuse.
- About 80% of 21 year olds that were abused as children met criteria for **at least one psychological disorder.**
- The estimated annual cost of child abuse and neglect in the United States for 2007 was **$104 billion.**
- Abused children are **25% more likely to experience teen pregnancy.**
- Abused teens are **3 times less likely** to practice safe sex, putting them at greater risk for STDs.

Child Abuse & Criminal Behavior

- 14% of all men in prison in the USA were abused as children
- 36% of all women in prison were abused as children
- Children who experience child abuse & neglect are 59% more likely to be arrested as a juvenile, 28% more likely to be arrested as an adult, and 30% more likely to commit violent crime.

Child Abuse Consequences

- Abused children are **25% more likely to experience teen pregnancy**
- Abused teens are **3 times less likely** to practice safe sex, putting them at greater risk for STDs

Child Abuse & Substance Abuse

- Children who have been sexually abused are **2.5 times more likely to abuse alcohol**

- Children who have been sexually abused are **3.8 times more likely to develop drug addictions**
- Nearly **two-thirds of the people** in treatment for drug abuse reported being abused as children"[14]

In the last 60 years, the US has spent about 20% of GDP on entitlements. The US is now 14 trillion in debt. If the US had had cheap, effective birth control, parenting classes, parenting licenses, trust funds, National Academies, and National Service maybe it would have turned out better. The United States would be a much nicer place to live for everybody and it would not be so heavily in debt.

There appear to be many abusive people in the US. These abusers are not just hurting their victims, they are almost ensuring that their victims will become abusers themselves one day. Followed to its natural conclusion, the US would become a nation full of abused people who in turn were abusing others. The more time and money government agencies, Churches, and Charities, have to spend on US citizens, the less time and money they have for suffering children in foreign nations.

There could be free birth control that only requires females to visit a clinic every 3 years. With the Internet, parenting classes, and parenting licenses would be extremely easy to coordinate. It would also be in everyone's best interests if every child bearing couple could establish a trust fund for each of their children. It would also behoove US citizens to limit the number of children they have to one or two depending on their financial status and other factors. Millions of children could one day attend one of the regionally located National Academies and go on to do their National Service requirement. If the US were to cut entitlement spending and military spending and pay down their debt, in 60 years, the US could have their national debt paid off. Their nation could be built upon a strong foundation of happily married couples and their one or two children. Every child could have civics training, teaching them respect for their nation and the planet as well. Every young adult would attend a National Academy where they would learn to be an exemplary citizen. Every 18 year old would get their life off to a good start by doing some form of National Service. Upon completion of their National Service, they could have accrued money for many types of schooling, or to start a business. They would also be able to access their trust funds

---

[14]   2007, Child Help: *National Child Abuse Statistics.* retrieved from *http://www. childhelp.Org/pages/statistics*

for such things as a down payment on a 3 bedroom, 2 bathroom "cookie cutter condo" on the monorail line. These simple measures would help create a strong foundation upon which the US could build a great nation, and even an empire.

As a result of all of these measures, US citizens could have much better childhoods, much better education, and more economic opportunity. Millions of US citizens could practice the concept of *noblesse oblige* and go out and do as much good as they could in the world. As we'll see in future chapters, the world could not only be "saved" within a century, it could be a utopia where every child has water, food, healthcare, shelter, education, and economic opportunity. The US could be the wealthiest, most diverse nation in the world, making it the perfect candidate to lead the way when it comes to repairing the planet. Instead of dominating the world with colonialism and imperialism, wealthier nations could practice altruism and Unitarianism. Maybe they would find out that a person catches more flies with honey than with vinegar.

Overpopulation and Birth Control

Worldwide, overpopulation is a pandemic, it is a root cause of extreme poverty. A possible solution might be matchstick size implants for females that provide birth control for 3 years. Young women would now be able to wait until they are mentally, physically, and financially prepared for the lifelong endeavor of parenting, before they have children. This could also allow females to limit the number of children they have in their lifetime. This could drastically alter the course of human history. A special program could offer this type of birth control free to all women. In exchange, women could agree to take parenting classes and receive a parenting license (which would benefit everyone) before they have children.

The world's population has doubled to 7 billion since 1960. It is scheduled to double again at least once this century. There could be over 10 billion people by 2050. The planet we are collectively ruining, if we keep destroying it, is not going to be able to sustain that many inhabitants.

Over a billion people live in poverty, extreme poverty, or absolute poverty. Some live on less than a dollar a day, and some do not even have that. They have to sit there starving to death while watching their own children and others die of dehydration, malnutrition, preventable diseases, war, murder, and other fates.

In 1979, following the death of Mao, the Chinese enacted a one-child policy. It is estimated that, 30 years later, the one-child policy has prevented 300 million births in China, the equivalent of the population of Europe.

There is currently a matchstick sized implant that will provide a female birth control for 3 years. It is safer and more effective than the shot, the pill, and condoms which can fail up to 25% of the time. Every woman worldwide, who is not practicing abstinence, and does not have a parenting license, could be getting these implants. The implants may be affordable to women in the developed world, but they continue to be cost prohibitive to women in poverty and developing nations who need them the most. Soon, generic versions of these implants will be available, making them much more affordable for women in poverty. In developing nations, Churches, Charities, Nonprofit Organizations, Government Agencies, philanthropists, and humanitarians could help pay for and implant the matchstick sized implants in the arm of every woman who is not ready for a child. Every woman in the world could one day have one of these matchstick sized implants that last for 3 years, helping to curb population explosion, especially in developing nations. This could be revolutionary!

Parenting Classes

Many future couples in the US could be introduced to each other using a Matchmaker Program similar to modern dating sites, but slightly more sophisticated and intricate. The program could do a very intensive and comprehensive study of each individual using a battery of tests and questionnaires. There could be I.Q. tests, emotional intelligence IQ test, personality inventories, skills assessments, physical tests, medical testing, aptitude tests, and many more. Users are then introduced to multiple potential life mates and have the opportunity to do live video chat and attend special singles events. When there is a positive match and two life partners pair off and get married, they could have a much greater likelihood of staying together than couples who have not been matched with the Matchmaker Program. Everyone who gets married using the Matchmaker Program can take advantage of one of many discounted honeymoon packages that the Matchmaker Program can afford to offer their participants. By buying vacations in bulk they can pass the savings on to the end consumer, in this case, the newlywed couple.

The next step in the process would be to acquire a parenting license, but first couples would have to pass their parenting classes. Parenting classes have been around for decades. Many of the current parenting classes are too expensive for some couples, and many of them are for people who are court ordered to take them. Now experts have a pretty clear idea of what works and what does not based on decades of research, statistical data, and empirical evidence. The best ideas could be synthesized and packaged into an easy, interactive, self paced parenting course that could be made available free online to prospective parents. The free, comprehensive parenting classes could cover everything from A to Z. It could be developed by the best and the brightest in every relevant field (prenatal to postnatal care, early childhood development, psychology, sociology, physical fitness, dieticians, and any others applicable). The prospective parents could benefit immensely from these courses. The courses can be taken online, in a classroom, or some combination of the two. There may even be field trips to places like the amusement park, or the zoo.

Once the prospective parents have done all of their homework and passed all of their classes, they could be ready to sit for the parenting exam. Upon passing this comprehensive, all day exam both parents will be granted their parenting license. In addition to being nationally certified, they could get something like a gift basket which could include free or discounted items they could need for the baby and maybe some gift cards from stores or restaurants. There could also be a party every week where newly licensed parents from all over the city get together for a social event that may include lectures, dinner, dancing, and more free gifts. Most importantly, there would be fellowship with other parents.

Various groups and Organizations could use this period to encourage prospective parents to join their groups or buy their products. They may also offer small gifts or gift cards as part of a public relations campaign. For example, a diaper company could give away a box of free diapers to every prospective parent who completes the parenting classes. A representative from a Nonprofit Organization could also inform parents that cloth diapers are cheaper, and better for the environment. Plus, plastic diapers are expensive and are the third largest source of trash in land fills. Prospective parents could also receive a coupon for some free baby formula as well as see a short presentation on the benefits of breast feeding.

One goal of the parenting classes would be to fully educate parents, and show them all of their options before they undertake the enormous responsibility of parenting. The parenting classes and exam could be an extremely intensive, comprehensive, series of courses, lectures, seminars, symposiums, conferences, and a final exam to test the preparedness of every parent. The curriculum and content would be designed by a panel of experts with a wide spectrum of expertise. The final model would be tested and retested before it was actually used to test anyone. There might be some beta groups and paid trials that would help work out any glitches in the system. Finally, they would complete and implement the best licensing system. Research will continue and each generation could have the benefit of inheriting a better system.

This would also be an opportunity for more fellowship, where prospective parents could interact with other licensees. There could definitely be a noticeable difference in the children whose parents got licensed and those who did not. Hopefully, this would encourage every couple to pursue a license, if it did not, there may be a movement to pass a law that would require all parents to get licensed.

Even people who already have one or more children, and have already passed the parenting licensure, may choose to, or be required to, take refresher classes and tests for each additional child. There could even be classes for older siblings, at the onsite daycare, that would help them prepare for the new addition to the family.

Parenting Licenses

The whole licensing process would be so challenging that passing the final exam, and obtaining the license could be one of the most memorable days in a person's life. It may mean even more to the couple than their wedding and honeymoon. Graduation parties would quickly become a tradition celebrated with parties and a much deserved vacation. Corporations could promptly offer discounted or even free products and services to the newly licensed couples. There could be a whole new section in the greeting card aisle for licensees.

Both parents would take the final parenting exam individually, and then part of it as a team. Each parenting team could typically have 1 to 3 children and the population should not rise. Within four generations, everyone alive could have been born to parents who had taken parenting classes, and were licensed, as well as mentally, physically, and financially prepared for the lifelong endeavor of parenting.

There could also be the option of getting an endorsement to adopt a child. Many parents could be encouraged to adopt or at least sponsor a child when possible. Every US couple could adopt or sponsor a child in another nation. What better PR campaign could there be to win the hearts and minds of the rest of the world, than millions of couples adopting and/or sponsoring children in other nations? That could be revolutionary!

Parenting Standard

A parenting standard could be the best way to ensure that every child is progressing properly in the pivotal years from conception, thru pre-kindergarten, and on through K-12. Once or twice a year, both parents would bring the child in for a physical and mental check up. The child would be tested in a number of ways to ensure they are developing properly mentally and physically.

The parents would be tested individually, and as a team, while the child was being tested elsewhere. Assuming the parent's and child/ren passed their tests, they would be given a list of suggestions for the next exam in 6 months to a year. If the child/ren or parent/s have anything they need to work on, they could be given instructions on what they can do to improve for their next exam. This way problems could never get out of control, they could be discovered and dealt with in a timely manner.

Optional Trust Fund

Parents planning to have children could be encouraged to establish a trust fund in the child's name. This trust fund could be added to at any time by anyone such as family members, Churches, Charities, or employers. The Fund could also be used as a reward or an incentive for such things as academic success or doing community service. Small contributions could be made to the Fund on the child's behalf that is performing well at something (wins an essay contest or has an exceptional science fair project or something), or is doing meritorious deeds in his or her community. Each quarter the child would get a statement showing how much was added to their account, and by whom, strengthening the bonds of family, and community.

This fund could also have a guaranteed minimum interest rate. For example, the government could match these funds 5% up to $5000. Any contributions to these funds with 5 cents per dollar up to $5000, for example. Any contributions to a fund could also be tax deductible. The fund would be guaranteed by the government up to a maximum amount.

Upon completion of their recommended National Service commitment, each child would "inherit" their Trust Fund. It could be paid out all at once, or over a period of time. They might get a bonus if they choose to "let it ride".

Summary

"If we are to have real peace, we must begin with the children." – **Mahatma Gandhi**[15]

"It takes a whole village to raise a child." – **African Proverb**[16]

It has been said that we do not inherit the world from our parents, we borrow it from our children. U.S. citizens did not take suitable care of their nation and they certainly did not take appropriate care of the planet, consequently, these could be the last of the "good old days". If the US were to change soon, it could be the dawn of a whole new era. What we do now could echo for eternity.

---

[15] http://thinkexist.com/quotation/if_we_are_to_teach_real_peace_in_ this_world-and/14282.html

[16] http://en.wikiquote.Org/wiki/African_proverbs

2

Necessity is the Mother of Invention

EVERY YEAR 2 million children die of dehydration, or related problems and complications, from a complete lack of water, or unsafe drinking water. This is a pandemic. It is estimated that every human's basic water needs could be met for a mere $30 billion. Today, it seems as if more people are concerned with hydrating their skin than helping hydrate children. The water currently available to most of the world's children could continue to be depleted as lakes, rivers, and groundwater from aquifers are drained completely dry. Humans currently spend over $100 billion on bottled water, which oftentimes, is no better, or is even worse than tap water, because bottled water has fewer regulations to comply with than tap water. The water bottling companies are also depleting lakes, rivers, and groundwater from aquifers. It could take centuries to replenish these aquifers.

The World Ocean (Antarctic, Arctic, Atlantic, Indian, and Pacific Oceans combined) contains 97% of the world's water, and there is currently 13,000+ desalination plants already, some pumping up to a billion liters of water per day. The solution to avoiding long term water shortages and massive desertification could be desalinating monumental amounts of water and pumping it inland to cities, and arid regions.

The World Ocean levels are expected to rise as high as 3 meters or about 9 feet by the end of this century. The previous estimates in inches apparently were not accurate. They did not consider that the land and water where the ice is melting are darker and attract more sunlight, speeding up the melting of the ice. There are certain other factors that could cause a sea level rise of 9 feet. The temperatures continually getting warmer does not help, it could raise the temperature of the water causing thermal expansion. This could not only wreak havoc on marine life, this could result in entire coastal cities being flooded.

Lack of water for agricultural purposes is making the problem even worse. Agriculture accounts for 70% of all the water consumed on earth. Lack of adequate water results in lower yields. More recently, pastureland and farmland has been drying up, creating desertification. Desertification has been claiming a dangerous amount of land. If the trend continues, it could have catastrophic results.

Instead of draining groundwater in aquifers, lakes, rivers, streams and the like, humans could start mass producing water desalination plants, and draining water from the rising oceans. This could be revolutionary!

Water Displacement Theory

There are currently over 13,000 water desalination plants in operation worldwide. Many are old and outdated and most of them are built completely different. Soon, new plants could be built that are capable of pumping 250 million gallons (or about 1 billion liters) of potable water out of the ocean every day.

The total volume of the World Ocean is 1,368,569,000,000,000,000 m3. It is predicted to rise by up to 3 meters or about 9 feet by the end of this century.

Humans could mass produce "desal" plants using the latest, greatest technology and begin pumping water as quickly as possible to every city, every arid region where desertification is creeping in, replenish rivers and lakes and even build new ones. The amount of water pumped out of the World Ocean would offset the worst possible estimate of a 3 meter (9 foot) rise in World Ocean levels.

A new Nonprofit Organization called the World Water Program could be established. They would begin mass producing desal plants. To help finance these plants, they could bottle some of the desalinated water in recycled plastic bottles. They could sell their new bottled water slightly cheaper than their competitors. Bottled water is a $100 billion a year industry. Oftentimes companies are taking water from aquifers, rivers, lakes, and streams that are drying up as a result. This water cannot be replenished as rapidly as it is being used. If people were to spend a sizable portion of that $100 billion on bottled water treated at desal plants, they would be helping save not just the aquifers, rivers, lakes, streams, and springs, they would be helping to save the world by reversing the rising sea levels. I think people would definitely be supportive of that when they make their bottled water purchase. Plus, the water would be better quality.

The World Water Program NPO (Nonprofit Organization) could design and build thousands of water desalination plants over the next few decades. Every Church, Charity, Nonprofit, and Government could contribute. What makes these thousands of desal plants different than all the others is that they are all the same. The exact same facility built the exact same way. Every part is mass produced, saving significantly on materials costs. The same general contracting firm that constructs these desal plants could be building the same desal plant every time. Each plant is the exact same, so these "Cookie Cutter Desal Plants" would be much cheaper to construct than their "one of a kind" predecessors were. In addition, every part used is mass produced and warehoused making maintenance over the decades much cheaper. These water desal plants are cheaper, and easier to maintain than the old "one of a kind" desal plants they are currently building. If there are changes and/or new technology, this NPO will be in a better position to adapt to changes than a contracting firm that has never built one before.

There would also need to be an intricate network of water pipelines from each plant to the surrounding areas. Billions of people could go from having no water to having an abundance of water. The more water they use, the better it is for the environment. They will be draining the World Ocean which could be rising up to 9 feet. Farms and pasture land would have an endless, inexhaustible supply of water enabling them to reverse the effects of desertification. They would be able to increase the number of arable acres of land, increasing the world's food output substantially. There could also be higher yields with better irrigation, further increasing the world food supply.

Desal plants could dot the coasts of every continent. They could be powered by an immense combination of solar, wind, and hydro power allowing them to be built "off-grid". They could have massive generators running on biodiesel. These titanic desalination plants could pump millions of gallons of water thousands of miles away, to its final destinations.

An abundance of water could mean that no human would ever die of dehydration or tainted water again. There could also be an abundance of food as well, insuring that no human could ever die from starvation again.

The costs of these desalination plants could be split between all nations. Each nation benefiting could contribute money, raw and unfinished materials, or labor to help fund the massive project. . All of the Nonprofits, Churches, and Charities could take their water budget and apply it to the construction and maintenance costs of the desal plants instead of building a few wells in random locations or other small projects, they could pitch in on this huge new project. The Nonprofit Org the "World Water Program", or a similar international agency, could take out long term loans to pay for the rest. The water could then be sold to farmers and other companies who use it to make a small profit. The proceeds from the sale of some of the water could help the Nonprofit Org pay off the loans. The WWP could purify water on-site and bottle it for sale on-site or nearby. The sale of this bottled water could help finance the whole program. In poorer nations, and locations where there is extreme poverty, the water could be free to those farmers, and others who cannot afford it. The water could be much cheaper than it is now because there could be an abundance of water, and the Nonprofit Org, the WWP could only need to make enough money to pay for the initial construction of the facilities, the pipeline network, and the daily operation and maintenance costs. This would make everything from municipal to irrigation water cheaper than ever before, and it could be given away free to the poor. A for profit company would charge much more for the water and probably would not consider giving it away to people dying of dehydration. The sole purpose of the Nonprofit Org the World Water Program, could be to supply desalinated water to every part of the world.

There could also be double hulled supermax tankers that could pull up near a desal plant, and fill up with desalinated water. They could then deliver it to any coastal location. These would be perfect for disaster relief. They could possibly even bottle the water right on board, as they are in transit to their target location.

Another option, would be trucks running on biodiesel with special food grade containers. They could fill up at the desal plant or anywhere along the pipeline network and truck the water to its final destination. Once complete, there should never be a shortage of water anywhere on earth again.

Highly concentrated salt water is a by product of desalinated water that typically gets pumped back into the ocean, and could possibly harm aquatic life and cause other problems. Scientists would have to find solutions such as salt pools where the water is evaporated by the sun leaving just the salt to dispose of. This could even be used to make sea salt or other products that could also be sold to help fund the WWP.

A combination of biodiesel, solar, wind, and hydro power could decrease the need for being connected to a power grid and save lots of money on electricity over the course of a century.

Where there was once desert, there could be farmland, pastureland, orchards and vineyards. Where once a child died every 20 seconds from lack of safe drinking water, there could be happy, healthy children, playing in pools with water slides.

Summary

In the future, Cookie Cutter Desalination Plants could:

1) provide safe drinking water to billions,
2) help reverse the effects of desertification,
3) provide much needed irrigation water for more arable land and higher agricultural yields, and
4) help lower rising sea levels

Where children once died of dehydration, there could be children playing in swimming pools. The more water they waste, the better it is for the environment. Where people are currently being charged high prices for water, there could be free unlimited potable water that can be used for better hygiene and sanitation. There could be rain in places that have not seen rain for generations. Humans could start reclaiming land lost to desertification. Where once there were deserts, there could be farmland, pastureland, orchards, and vineyards. Aquifers could have a chance to get replenished over the coming decades, and, maybe most importantly, the sea level would not rise as high as predicted.

3

Make Hunger History By 2050

A N ADULT DIES every second either directly or indirectly from hunger. A child dies either directly or indirectly from hunger every 5 seconds. That would mean 16,000 children die every day. that is 6 million every year. The statistics are staggering:

GLOBAL HUNGER

- 925 million people do not have enough to eat – more than the populations of USA, Canada and the European Union; *(Source: FAO news release, 14 September 2010)*
- 98 percent of the world's hungry live in developing countries; *(Source: FAO news release, 2010)*
- Asia and the Pacific region is home to over half the world's population and nearly two thirds of the world's hungry people; (Source: *FAO news release*, 2010)
- Women make up a little over half of the world's population, but they account for over 60 percent of the world's hungry. *(Source: Strengthening efforts to eradicate hunger . . ., ECOSOC, 2007)*

- 65 percent of the world's hungry live in only seven countries: India, China, the Democratic Republic of Congo, Bangladesh, Indonesia, Pakistan and Ethiopia. *(Source: FAO news release, 2010)*

CHILD HUNGER

- More than 70 percent of the world's 146 million underweight children under age five years live in just 10 countries, with more than 50 per cent located in South Asia alone; *(Source: Progress for Children: A Report Card on Nutrition, UNICEF, 2006)*
- 10.9 million children under five die in developing countries each year. Malnutrition and hunger-related diseases cause 60 percent of the deaths; *(Source: The State of the World's Children, UNICEF, 2007)*
- The cost of undernutrition to national economic development is estimated at US$20-30 billion per annum; *(Source: Progress for Children: A Report Card on Nutrition, UNICEF, 2006)*
- One out of four children – roughly 146 million – in developing countries are underweight; *(Source: The State of the World's Children, UNICEF, 2007)*
- Every year WFP feeds more than 20 million children in school feeding programmes in some 70 countries. In 2008, WFP fed a record 23 million children. (Source: WFP School Feeding Unit)

MALNUTRITION

- It is estimated that 684,000 child deaths worldwide could be prevented by increasing access to vitamin A and zinc *(Source: WFP Annual Report 2007)*
- Undernutrition contributes to 53 percent of the 9.7 million deaths of children under five each year in developing countries. *(Source: Under five deaths by cause, UNICEF, 2006)*
- Lack of Vitamin A kills a million infants a year *(Source: Vitamin and Mineral Deficiency, A Global Progress Report, UNICEF)*
- Iron deficiency is the most prevalent form of malnutrition worldwide, affecting an estimated 2 billion people. Eradicating iron deficiency can improve national productivity levels by as much as 20 percent. *(Source: World Health Organization, WHO Global Database on Anaemia)*

- Iron deficiency is impairing the mental development of 40-60 percent children in developing countries *(Source: Vitamin and Mineral Deficiency, A Global Progress Report, p2, UNICEF)*
- Vitamin A deficiency affects approximately 25 percent of the developing world's pre-schoolers. It is associated with blindness, susceptibility to disease and higher mortality rates. It leads to the death of approximately 1-3 million children each year. *(Source: UN Standing Committee on Nutrition. World Nutrition Situation 5th report. 2005)*
- Iodine deficiency is the greatest single cause of mental retardation and brain damage. Worldwide, 1.9 billion people are at risk of iodine deficiency, which can easily be prevented by adding iodine to salt *(Source: UN Standing Committee on Nutrition. World Nutrition Situation 5th report. 2005)*

FOOD & HIV/AIDS

- In the countries most heavily affected, HIV has reduced life expectancy by more than 20 years, slowed economic growth, and deepened household poverty. *(Source: 2008 UNAIDS Global Report on the AIDS Epidemic)*
- In sub-Saharan Africa alone, the epidemic has orphaned nearly 12 million children aged under 18 years. *(Source: 2008 UNAIDS Global Report on the AIDS Epidemic)*.
- WFP and UNAIDS project that it could cost on average US $0.70 cents per day to nutritionally support an AIDS patient and his/her family. *(Source: Cost of Nutritional Support for HIV/AIDS Projects, WFP, July 2008)*
- Assistance for orphans and vulnerable children is estimated at US$0.31 per day. *(Source: Cost of Nutritional Support for HIV/AIDS Projects, WFP, July 2008)*[17]

We live in a world where 20% of the world's population consumes 80% of its resources. It is estimated that only $175 billion per year could make sure the world's impoverished have their basic needs met. The United States currently spends only about $25 billion on foreign aid. The US also spends about $685 billion on military spending, about

---

[17] *Hunger Stats | WFP | United Nations World Food Programme* ... (n.d.). Retrieved from http://www.wfp.Org/hunger/stats

$650 billion going out for food and beverages, about $380 billion on computers and electronics, about $185 billion on entertainment and recreation (gambling, sports, concerts, strip clubs, etc.), about $9 billion on films and music, and the list is endless. If individuals and corporations would just give a little more each year, we could end world poverty, or at least make sure the impoverished had their basic needs met.

In the same vein, if 3 million US farmers can grow enough grain to feed 2 billion people, imagine what the possibilities would be if the whole world was irrigated, and using the latest agricultural technology and equipment. The US could package everything that people in poverty need: water, food, medicine, clothing, tents, education materials, toys for the children, solar panels, small electronics, a video camera to upload a daily journal, and much more. They could stamp the American flag and USA all over everything, and send it to every impoverished area in the world. They could have a fleet of Boeing C-17A Globemaster III cargo planes painted with stars and stripes coming in low and slow to drop the supplies. Americans will once again be the hero's in children's eyes. If a friend in need is a friend indeed, America would make millions of friends for life (FFL) overnight. By this time next year, millions of people could be waving little American flags (included in their aid package) and filming it with the included cameras.

In Haiti, the kids had resorted to eating mud cakes before US aid workers arrived with supplies. Those children could have a positive image of the United States until they die and they could probably teach their children to have a positive impression too. What better public relations could there be than the US sending volunteers and supplies to places like Haiti.

As a result of the construction of thousands of mass produced water desalination plants and a comprehensive network of water pipelines, the world could be "flooded" with an unlimited supply of water for the rest of history. This unlimited water could significantly increase the amount of arable land. The unlimited irrigation water could also lead to higher yields per acre or hectare. Where there was once desert, there could be farms, ranches, orchards, and vineyards. The world's food supply could increase dramatically.

The same way the water desalination plants were mass produced and built to last centuries, food processing facilities could be mass produced and strategically placed all over the globe. A Nonprofit Org devoted to getting every child a glass of milk per day, similar to India's "White revolution" could achieve its goal by 2050. Nonprofit Orgs devoted to growing, producing, processing grains, fruits, vegetables, beef, dairy, chicken, pork, fish, etc. could be mass producing facilities all over the planet. These facilities could offer better working conditions, and a better living wage for the employees. By holding costs down and taking profit out of the equation, they could easily afford to feed billions of people that would have never gotten fed before. Together, the human race can make hunger history by 2050.

One example of this concept in action would be going to the world's most productive chicken processing facilities, seeing what they are doing right, and observing what other chicken production facilities are doing wrong. Design the ultimate chicken processing facility and mass produce it several thousand times. Strategically place the facilities all over the world. These facilities could be owned by a Nonprofit Organization. There could be better working conditions, a better living wage for employees, and a cheaper product, saving the consumer some money. These new NPO's would put people and the planet and the customer before profit.

Once 1000's of these world's largest, most efficient chicken production and processing facilities are constructed, there could be an abundance of chicken. The chicken can then be cooked and packaged in cans, pouches, bags of chicken jerky, dehydrated #10 cans of cubed chicken, and any other form of packaging that could give it a longer shelf life. There could still be plenty of fresh chicken for consumers within the shipping area of the facility. Biodiesel/Electric refrigerated food trucks would deliver the fresh chicken everywhere within a certain mile radius. Then another Nonprofit Org can do the same thing with beef. The NPO can buy or lease ranch land and build feed lots and the best meat packing facilities money can buy. They could eventually be the world's primary supplier of beef, both fresh and preserved.

An NPO that specializes in nothing but supplying the world with the cheapest pork could buy or lease land in every region. They could set up 1000's of the largest and most efficient pork production/processing plants in the world, and ship pork to markets via their global distribution network. They could be unsurpassed in the amount of pork they can process. The NPO is not making any profit, and they are mass producing everything, so the final price could be a fraction of what it is now.

When it comes to seafood, there is a huge problem. The oceans are being over fished. In 1900, the oceans contained at least six times more fish than today. Stocks of large predatory fish such as tuna and cod are nearly depleted. It also takes much more effort to catch a ton of fish than it did 100 years ago. There are 3 times as many ships, yet the average catch is lower than in 1900. Millions of peoples livelihoods depend on the fishing industry, billions of peoples diets depend on fish as a source of nutrients.

However, with aquaculture, fish like tilapia and salmon can be farm raised. An NPO could bring in the expensive equipment, pay some locals to operate it, and they could have the worlds largest, most efficient sources of fresh fish. They could mass produce these "fish farms" and all of the equipment needed for them. They could then be strategically located just about anywhere.

For ocean caught fish, the NPO could make the world's largest, most efficient, fishing ships and have limitations on where they can harvest fish, and the size of their catches. They can process the fish right on the boat, and flash freeze them until they get to shore where they could send them for canning or further processing. They could also distribute them fresh to the end consumer who could expect to pay much less for them because the NPO that brought them in is not making a profit.

There could be such an abundance of food, almost everyone could be able to afford it. For those who can not afford food, (and there should be fewer people every year), there could be free subsistence food giveaway locations strategically located in every city on Earth, as well as many rural sites.

Like everything, this would take a concerted effort on behalf of millions of individuals. If it is done right, it could eliminate all deaths as a result of dehydration and starvation. This could be revolutionary!

Peak Soil

Another concern humans need to be aware of, is the diminishing topsoil, which is the top several inches of soil that is crucial to farming. It takes about 500 years to form an inch, so humans would be wise to conserve it. It can easily get washed away with heavy rain, blown away when it is dry (like the dust bowl in the mid-US from 1930-36 (the dirty thirties)), and it can gradually get depleted with over use. Soil degradation is the result of many factors including, overgrazing, deforestation, agricultural activities, overexploitation for fuel wood, and industrialization. The population is supposed to double again, except this time, the amount of land suitable for agriculture is declining. Soil erosion is fast becoming one of the worlds worst problems.

"Experts predict that crop yields could be halved within thirty to fifty years if erosion continues at present rates. Soil erosion is not unique to Africa but is occurring worldwide. The phenomenon is being called *Peak Soil.* Large scale factory farming techniques are jeopardizing humanity's ability to grow food in the present and in the future. Without efforts to improve soil management practices, the availability of arable soil could become increasingly problematic.

Some Soil Management techniques
1. No-till farming
2. Keyline Design
3. Growing wind breaks to hold the soil
4. Incorporating Organic matter back into the fields
5. Stop using chemical fertilizers (which contain salt)"[18]

Peak Soil may be an even greater threat to humanity than Peak Oil. If the soil continues to get abused, the topsoil could get depleted, and agricultural yields could not be as bountiful as they used to be. Soil, like oil, is a non-renewable resource. Unlike oil, however, there is no new technology like biodiesel, electric cars, wind and solar power, electric trains, or some new invention, waiting to replace soil when it runs out. In 1937, Franklin Roosevelt said, The nation that destroys its soils destroys itself."[19] The United States and most other nations seem to be doing just that.

These new NPO's discussed earlier in the chapter could educate farmers on sustainable agriculture. They can also sell, lease, or give them new and used equipment and show them how to use it properly. They could supply them with unlimited Organic fertilizer made at regional Organic fertilizer factories. Massive amounts of water could be getting piped in from the desal plants on the coasts in order to fully irrigate farm and pastureland, plus provide life saving water for humans and animals. There could be regionally located International Cities, (discussed in Chapter 4) that would have storehouses for every type of grain from

---

[18] *Sustainable agriculture - Wikipedia, the free encyclopedia.* (n.d.). Retrieved from http://en.wikipedia.Org/wiki/Sustainable_agriculture

[19] http://www.brainyquote.com/quotes/quotes/f/franklind396994.html

regional farms, or shipped in from elsewhere. They could also function as a seed bank and lease equipment.

Organic Fertilizers

In addition to water and sunlight, plants need nitrogen, phosphorous, and potassium. As if peak oil and peak soil were not enough to worry about, now it is estimated that America only has about 30 years worth of phosphorus left, resulting in the term **peak phosphorus.** They could then have to start purchasing it elsewhere, such as from Morocco, at ridiculously high prices. The world supply should run out this century, and there is no real known substitute yet discovered.

The way food is raised, processed, and distributed now is inhumane, inefficient, and bad for the environment.

Three ways humans could use Organic fertilizer and save phosphorus are 1) vermicomposting leftover food; 2) humanure; 3) and resomation.

All leftover food from every restaurant, home, and building could be collected in certain containers and picked up on a regular basis. The excess food waste just beginning to rot is the perfect food for the millions of red worms at the vermicomposting facility. The red worms turn all of the rotten food into one of the best Organic fertilizers on earth. The worm castings can be gathered and mixed with the humanure and the resomated remains of the regions deceased to create a 3 in 1 Organic super fertilizer.

Humanure is kind of what it sounds like, human waste, urine and fecal matter. The sewer system of every major city could be routed to a treatment facility where black and grey water could be processed to make a humanure liquid fertilizer. That could then be mixed with worm castings (from the vermicomposting) and the resomated remains of the deceased to create an Organic super fertilizer.

Eventually, all new buildings could have their grey water recycled on-site and pumped back up to the bathrooms and used to flush two stage toilets that have one button for #1 and a second button for #2. Then the blackwater would be routed to a centralized facility that would treat the blackwater (feces, urine) that was flushed down the toilet with the grey water, and add it to the super fertilizer.

Every dead body can be turned into a small quantity of green-brown liquid through a chemical process called resomation. This liquid can then be mixed with the worm castings and the humanure to create the world's greatest super fertilizer.

Summary

One day, there could be giant automated farms growing crops like rice, for example. They would take a super strain of rice known for it's large size and quick growth. They could have millions of trays of a growing medium like rock wool cubes and an overhead planting machine would deposit one grain in each cube. The trays would then be lowered into the "paddies," or shallow pools of water. The water in the "paddies" could be a nutrient and fertilizer rich solution that helps the rice grow as large as possible in a short period of time. When ready to harvest, the trays are lifted and another overhead machine comes along and collects and dries the rice and discards the rest. There could be 4 or more such crops annually per automated farm. The elements would not be an issue, nor would pests, or other typical problems associated with growing in the wild. There could also be automated vertical farms using hydroponics, super seeds, super fertilizer, artificial lighting, and other technology to generate several "super" crops per year. These new "Super Farms" could be located in just about any climate on just about any terrain. About 90% of all food consumed by humans comes from just 15 plants and 8 animals that can one day be mass produced to feed every person on earth.

About 70% of all water used by humans is for irrigation, with only about 20% being used by humans for drinking, cooking, cleaning, and other uses. All humans have to do is desalinate water, and use solar, wind, and hydro power to pump it to every part of the planet. They can then apply the Organic super fertilizer, grow the 15 plants and raise the 8 animals and process them in large mass produced facilities with hyper efficiency and there could be an abundance of food for all of humanity, even if the population doubles which it is supposed to do at least once this century. This could be revolutionary!

4

Health is Wealth

ALTHOUGH APPROXI-MATELY 10.5 million children under 5 years of age still die every year in the world, progress has been made since 1970, when the figure was more than 17 million. Infectious and parasitic diseases remain the major killers of children in the developing world, partly as a result of the HIV/AIDS epidemic. Although notable success has been achieved in certain areas (for example, polio), *communicable diseases still represent 7 out of the top 10 causes of child deaths, and account for about 60% of all child deaths.* Overall, the ten leading causes represent 86% of all child deaths. (see Table 1.1)

Table 1.1 Leading causes of death in children in developing countries, 2002

Rank	Cause	Numbers	% of all deaths
1.	Perinatal conditions	2,375,000	23.1
2.	Lower respiratory infections	1,856,000	18.1
3.	Diarrhoeal diseases	1,566,000	15.2
4.	Malaria	1,098,000	10.7
5.	Measles	551,000	5.4

6.	Congenital anomalies	386,000	3.8
7.	HIV/AIDS	370,000	3.6
8.	Pertussis	301,000	2.9
9.	Tetanus	185,000	1.8
10.	Protein-energy malnutrition	138,000	1.3
	Other Causes	1,437,000	14.0
	Total	**10,263,000**	100.0[20]

International Clinics

Every one of the diseases on that list is preventable, and yet we lose 6 million children per year. Plus, all of the children who are being orphaned by the loss of one or both parents, and should be in everybody's prayers. There were 16 million children (mostly in sub-Saharan Africa) orphaned when they lost one or both parents to AIDS, a disease that is 100% preventable, 0% curable.

A Nonprofit Org designed specifically to aid in the prevention of disease, with a mission to end child suffering and death by 2050 could open a chain of thousands of strategically placed clinics in every major city, with some rural locations as well, especially in developing nations. They could offer a free annual checkup for women and children. Every year, women and their children would either go to their nearest clinic or in the event there is not one nearby, they could be picked up by biodiesel/electric bus and taken to their nearest clinic. By using this kind of preventive medicine, humans can start stopping problems before they start.

Upon reaching the clinic, mothers could be registered and have all of their information entered into a database to help researchers compile statistics. Then they could have breakfast and wait in comfortable waiting rooms with games and toys for the children and lots of reading material for the adults. Throughout the day, every woman and child would receive a comprehensive physical exam and have any necessary medications (antibiotics, for example) given to the mother and child/ren free of charge. In addition, every woman would receive a form of birth control effective for up to 3 years. This would also be free of charge to them. The children could get all of their immunizations while they are there getting their checkup. They would also be served lunch and

[20] *WHO | Chapter 1: Global Health: today's challenges.* (n.d.). Retrieved from http://www.who.int/whr/2003/chapter1/en/index2.html/target

dinner. Between meals, the mothers could sit through informational seminars while the children play in specially designed, educational play areas for children in each particular region. The children may also watch educational movies and documentaries or play educational games.

At the end of the day, every woman and child would be given a biodegradable backpack for each family member. A typical backpack may include several packets of multi-flavored, fortified powdered milk packets, several packs of multi-flavored oatmeal packets, several packs of multi-flavored ramen noodles with vegetable packets, some protein pills, nutrition bars, anti-diarrheals, re-hydration salts, medicines both prescription and over the counter, a mosquito net if they do not have one already, some toiletry items such as soap and toothpaste and a toothbrush, cleaning products like a pouch of bleach, or anything they might need in their region that could fit in a backpack. All of the items should be light enough for a woman to carry, the small children could get their own little backpack with some food and medicine, as well as a few little toys. For many, the clinic could be within walking distance. For most, they could take the biodiesel/electric bus back to where they were picked up.

In the video presentations, parents (mostly mothers) could be shown the benefits of having only one or two children. They could also be given parenting advice from experts in the fields of early childhood development that are from their region. There could even eventually be a program where they could take a parenting class every time they visit the clinic. Once they have passed every class and were ready to be a parent, they could stop taking the birth control until after they have their child, and then they can start the whole process over. This way, every pregnancy is planned, and the mother and child have the best healthcare available. This could drastically reduce the number of deaths for children under 5, it would also help keep the world population from doubling again so soon. These clinics are definitely a worthwhile investment for humanity. Within a few generations, thousands of these clinics could be helping to stabilize the population growth in developing nations. The clinics could also be able to collect data about every individual in their coverage area.

Summary

Someone once described love as staying up all night with a sick child. Every year 10.5 million children die, mostly from preventable causes.

Millions more are orphaned, especially in Sub-Saharan Africa. Nobody seems to care about these children, not even their own mothers who routinely abandon them. There is a saying, before we heal others, we must first heal ourselves. It's hard to help others if we can't help ourselves. There's millions of US citizens going to food shelves. Meanwhile, 6 million children die of starvation. If ever there was a nation, that could lead the way, and save humanity and the planet, the US is it. If the citizens of the United States are living longer, healthier, happier, more prosperous lives and teaching their children to do the same, they could be in a better position to help others in need, particularly children in other nations. There could be millions of wealthy US citizens working together to end world poverty and improve the quality of life for children in every part of the world. With help from people and Organizations who care, dehydration, starvation, and preventable diseases will no longer claim millions of little lives.

5

Cookie Cutter Construction

THE ADVANTAGES OF "cookie cutter" construction are numerous. It involves constructing virtually the same home or building several times in order to save time and money on design, materials, and labor, as well as keep future maintenance costs low. Everyone has seen tract homes, it's the same basic concept but on a grander scale.

About the only possible criticism of cookie cutter construction projects is that they all look similar. They certainly can, but it's not too hard to give them individuality. It could just as easily be argued, that building a million completely different buildings that look completely different and function completely different, that are more expensive to design, and build, and maintain, is insane.

By having one basic design, possibly with multiple variations, the design costs of building a 1000 buildings is 1/1000 of what it would be to build 1000 "one of a kind" homes or buildings.

The next advantage to "cookie cutter" construction is the savings in material costs. As the worlds resources dwindle, some building materials are in high demand and high materials prices can drive the final cost of any building project "through the roof". If there were over a million "one of a kind" buildings built in the next century, the materials costs would be astronomical. If many of these buildings were mass produced "cookie cutter" buildings, there would be a significant reduction in materials costs. There would be far less waste, and materials could be purchased in bulk, and in many cases made out of recycled materials. There are a lot of excellent new products that could be bought in bulk and used for cookie cutter construction that may have been cost prohibitive for individual projects. Contrary to what some people might think, cookie cutter homes and buildings can actually be designed and built better and use better materials than their one of a kind counterparts. They could look better, be designed and built better, and could be made with better quality materials. They could be constructed by firms and people that know exactly what they are doing because they have done it thousands of times, and they could be easier and cheaper to maintain in the long run.

With cookie cutter construction, there could be highly reputable general contractors who recruit the best and the brightest employees and pay them well and give them a lifetime career, not just a temporary job. These employees would be paid a fair, living wage with a comprehensive benefits package. They would travel around the nation and the world overseeing the construction of thousands of projects. The subcontractors could have the same high standards as the general contractors, and their career employees would typically live in the area of the projects being constructed. It would be the same men and women, building the same homes and buildings, thousands of times, all over the world. This would be the great career path for anyone in any building trade. They would literally be making history.

The new goal of cookie cutter construction should be to build millions of buildings that last for centuries, instead of cheap homes and buildings that don't stand the test of time. People may have to be willing to pay a little more for quality, but it will be worth it in the end.

Since every part of these homes and buildings is mass produced, it would be easy enough to calculate the life span of each part of the structure, and mass produce extra parts accordingly, and warehouse them regionally, so they could be shipped out the same day if the need arose. Most of the cookie cutter mass produced homes and buildings would last over a century. The building owners may also contract with a long term maintenance firm that would offer full time careers to many of the workers who constructed the homes and buildings.

The net result is the consumer is getting a home or building built better, by the best professionals, with the best materials, for a lot less than a similar one of a kind construction. Plus, the maintenance costs are far less over the lifetime of the structure. it is a win-win-win situation where all of humanity benefits immensely. This is revolutionary!

Cookie Cutter Industrial Cities

The cookie-cutter Industrial Cities could create millions of careers. Employers could offer an all inclusive compensation package that would allow them to pay employees less in wages, but offer them more in benefits. The employer could pay them primarily with benefits that the employer could provide more cheaply than the individual worker and his/her family could purchase on their own. The employers could be for profit or Nonprofit Organizations that have facilities in one or more Industrial Cities.

These "Cities" could have several factories, warehouses, office buildings, employee housing, dining halls (with 24 hour international food court and buffet), stores, health/dental/vision clinics, hospitals, schools, recreation areas, parks, and just about everything an ordinary city would have. All buildings would be mass produced and clustered together so they could be connected by tunnels, skyways and moving sidewalks, reducing the need for private transportation.

As part of their compensation, workers could live on-site, in nice furnished apartments, all of their utilities could be paid, they would have no transportation expenses, they could enjoy a 24 hour international food court buffet that delivers around the clock. Employees would enjoy free health, dental, and vision for their family (including cosmetic surgery and dentistry, laser eye surgery, and more). There would also be a free Pre K-8 academy on-site. Other amenities may include a store that sells everything the employees need, and most of what they want, much more affordably than they would find it elsewhere. There could be indoor and outdoor pools with water slides for the kids and hot tubs for the adults, as well as eucalyptus steam rooms and saunas. A day spa. A 24 hour fitness center with the latest, greatest equipment. They could also have a fleet of shuttles and buses running on biodiesel that would take employees and their families anywhere they need or want to go, including on group vacations. The employees would only make a small monetary wage. Their benefits package, however, could make their entire compensation worth more than if they were making a larger wage and trying to pay for rent, utilities, and transportation. Plus, having to buy food and cook and clean. The employees would also save on their families health, dental and vision expenses. In addition, they would pay much less to take their family to do fun stuff with other families, and go on group vacations.

The industrial cities would be a win-win-win situation.

Cookie Cutter Group Homes

The problem of homelessness is becoming an epidemic not just in developing nations, but in developed nations like the US, as well. With the population scheduled to double again this century, housing shortages can only get worse. One way to deal with homelessness would be to mass produce eco-friendly group homes. The exteriors would be the same, and the interiors could be set up to fit the particular needs of each building and its future residents. The materials costs would be a fraction of those for "one-of-a-kind" buildings. Labor costs would be much less as well, because they are using the same general contractors for every building, and much of the building is prefabricated. In areas where several of these cookie cutter homes are going up, the same local subcontractors can be used to cut labor costs. There might even be the option of giving future residents the opportunity to earn "sweat equity" by helping around the constructionsite.

These group homes could be the same shell building, but the interior could be used for homeless men, battered women, handicapped people, assisted living for the elderly, home for the deaf and/or blind, student housing, single mothers, priests and nuns, veterans, retirees, assisted living for the infirm, alcohol and drug rehabilitation centers, half-way houses for recently released inmates on parole, low wage earners, refugees, or even youth hostels. The typical layout could be several upper floors of furnished (bed, dresser, desk, and TV with cable) sleeping rooms with a large bathroom and kitchen on each floor. The earth-bermed sub floors could be for heated underground parking with 440V electrical outlets for biodiesel/electric car charging. The basement may also house such amenities as a pool with hot tubs or a theater with one of those movie theater style, popcorn makers with the melted, butter flavored oil. The main floor would have a security monitored entrance and lobby. The entire building could have state-of-the-art security with cameras everywhere. Some facilities may want more security than others. There could also be a store that purchases everything the residents might need in bulk and sells it at cost. A food court, typically with a buffet, sized proportionately according to the building's population. There could also be a health, dental, and vision clinic offering cheap or even free services for the residents. The kitchens, if there are any, on the upper floors could be small with a few appliances, a microwave, and cupboards. Most of the residents would eat in the food court. The main kitchen on the ground floor would be the same for every building. It would consist of the most modern equipment available mass produced specifically for the group homes. All of the food served could be mass produced for thousands of the same group homes as well, which would save on operating costs.

These group homes could be mass produced and ultra-durable with every part that could possibly need replacing warehoused at a regional facility. Each region would have their own parts warehouse, so anytime something needed to be replaced, it could be delivered by a truck running on biodiesel within a few days, saving even more carbon. Construction costs would be far less than if each building were built separately, and maintenance and operating costs would be much lower, as well. The goal would be zero-carbon emissions, or maybe even better if they have an attached greenhouse, farm, orchard, or vineyard, for example. There could also be solar hot water heaters and photovoltaic (PV) panels (for electricity) on the roof, as well as some wind turbines. Brick and/or adobe and/or stucco exterior with new high R-value windows and new high R-value insulation would help maintain carbon neutrality. The interior walls can be made of papercrete from recycled paper and the floors can have rubber mats made from recycled auto tires. All of the kitchen and bathroom equipment is mass produced for thousands of buildings. The grey water could be recycled and treated on-site and used to flush the two-stage toilets (1 button for #1, a second button for #2) in every bathroom. The black water could be treated and used as "humanure" fertilizer for landscaping or pumped to a central facility that takes all of the blackwater in the area and turns it into fertilizer for nearby farms in the form of "humanure". There could also be a community garden with compost piles for leaves and brush, and even a vermicomposting bin where all of the food waste could be fed to red worms, who would turn it into the one of the best Organic fertilizers there is.

Since many of the residents could be indigent, there could be a plethora of jobs on-site that they can do to pay their rent. If the same Nonprofit Org owns and operates dozens or even hundreds of these structures, each individual would only have to pay a few dollars a day for rent, food, and other amenities. There might be a temp labor agency on-site that would take workers to and from their places of employment every day. The temp job workers could stop by the kitchen on their way to the biodiesel shuttle and pick up a bag lunch. The residents could also make money from raising food for a farmer's market, or other unique inventive ways. They may have a Sunday Social on-site where the residents and/or staff, prepare a breakfast for members of the surrounding community. They could charge a nominal fee per plate. The residents could also give a presentation about a particular charitable cause, and at the end of the presentation, guests could choose to text a donation to a Nonprofit Organization to help the cause they just learned about. The residents who prepare and serve the meal could use the money they earn per plate to put towards operating costs, some group activities, new equipment, or other things they may need or want.

The residents rent could be extremely cheap because of the low design, construction, operation, and maintenance costs and the vast number (over a million) residents in 1000's of facilities nationwide. They could either pay their rent if they could afford it, work it off on-site, or have it paid for them by the government, Nonprofit Organizations, Charities, Churches, family, or some other source.

These near zero-carbon emission buildings could change the way millions of people live both nationally and internationally.

They could be owned and operated by Nonprofit Orgs. These NPO's could be helping the residents with much more than shelter. There would be schooling, a chapel, a library, counseling, group fellowship activities, and many other things that would help people in their particular position. Some residents may get money from the government, but the facility should not cost the taxpayers a penny, it could even save them money.

Cookie Cutter Mobile Homes/Parks

They say those who do not learn from history are doomed to repeat it. The mobile home park is a brilliant concept that could be improved upon. These cookie cutter mobile home parks could be much nicer than anything existing today. A Nonprofit Organization could buy millions of acres of land in and around every major metropolitan area. They could establish thousands of these new mobile home oases all over the nation. Each facility would have every amenity imaginable all constructed from mass produced parts, and made and prefabricated in the region, creating much needed careers for US citizens.

Each facility would have amenities like an indoor/outdoor pool with water slides for the kids and hot tubs, eucalyptus steam rooms. There could also be a fitness room with the latest and greatest equipment. There could be a day spa, beauty parlor, and barber shop. There could be an international food court with dozens of cheap restaurants that deliver. Each park could also have a health, dental, and vision clinic and pharmacy on-site. In addition, there could be a general store that purchases everything residents may need in bulk and sells it to them at cost. These parks could be owned by a Nonprofit Org, so the annual fee to pay for grounds maintenance, snow removal, and other necessary tasks, is significantly less compared to what most for profit parks are currently charging. This could mean much better parks and much smaller individual lot fees.

The surrounding area could be used for a small hobby farm, community garden, orchard, vineyard, even some livestock, horses, and ponies. Depending on the location and the climate, there is an endless number of possibilities for what they can have in or near the parks. There could also be a combination day care, pre-K, and K-8 academy where students could prepare for their future studies at the National Academy.

Tens of thousands of homes could be constructed regionally and shipped to these parks on trucks running on biodiesel. The homes are an ultra modern version of the mobile homes of today, with solar hot water and photovoltaic (PV) panels (for solar electricity) on the roof. They could work in combination with new, ultra-efficient appliances such as hot water heaters, refrigerators, electric ranges and ovens, laundry machines, and central air units that oxygenate, ionize, filter, and even scent the air. All of these appliances will be specifically designed for use in these new, ultramodern mobile homes. Each home would also have high R-value insulation and double glazed windows. These homes would be comparable in price to current mobile homes, but they could last longer, thus having better resale value. Plus, there would be no initial sales mark-up because they could be manufactured by a Nonprofit Org. They would also be much cheaper to operate and maintain, as well. Furthermore, there would be no lot rent because the parks are owned and operated by a Nonprofit Org, there would only be a small annual park fee.

There could also be a small water treatment facility in the park that recycles all of the grey water, and pumps it back to the homes to be used to flush the 2 stage toilets. They could even channel the waste water from the entire park to a nearby facility where it could be turned into fertilizer.

Even the best of the mobile homes being produced today, and the nicest parks in the nation, could not compare to these future homes and parks. Plus, they are eco-friendly and strive to be carbon neutral.

Cookie Cutter Condominiums

The cookie cutter condominium could be the most common form of housing in the future. They can house more people, and offer them more amenities, in less space, more efficiently, for less money, than any other housing option. They could be much less expensive, yet better quality, and with better amenities than any "one of a kind" condos being built today. All of these condos could attempt to be carbon neutral, thus reducing each inhabitants carbon footprint. They could be owned and operated by Nonprofit Orgs instead of for-profit corporations, making them even more affordable. These cookie cutter condos could offer people that would never have been able to own property, the opportunity to buy their own condo. A billion plus people buying cookie cutter condos, and keeping the condos in their family for over a century, could have a profound effect on humanity. Instead of paying rent, world citizens could be building equity in their own property. A great leap forward for mankind. This could be revolutionary!

These ultra-modern condominiums would be designed to be affordable, efficient, with all the amenities and net zero carbon emissions. What they would sacrifice in opulent luxury, they would make up for in amenities. This perfect design could then be mass produced, and constructed a million times over the course of a century, with a few minor changes and retrofits.

Each building can be custom tailored to the end users specifications, with thousands of different configurations available. Besides being different colors and having different accents, each building could have a unique mixture of residential, office, retail, restaurant, recreation, and open space. Most of the exteriors could be about the same, possibly with a little variety.

The basic unit condo could be a 3 bedroom and 2 bathroom apartment home perfect for a family of four. Everything in the building, inside and out could be mass produced and built thousands of times. This is much more efficient than building thousands of luxurious one of a kind buildings, each one unique and expensive, using different designs, different contractors, and different materials. Every building could have the same or similar amenities or they could be attached to other buildings that do. Each building could have certain amenities that residents in all of the connected buildings could share, for example: a day spa, an indoor/outdoor pool with waterslide for the kids, hot tubs, eucalyptus steam room and sauna for adults, and a high tech fitness center. There could also be an international food court that delivers just about everything, within minutes (fresh coffee and bakery every morning, lunch to go, dinner for the whole family without having to cook and clean). Also onsite, would be a daycare, pre-k, and K-8 Academy with a plethora of extracurricular activities. A health, dental, and vision clinic performs all basic services at low cost, also available would be such things as cosmetic dentistry, laser eye surgery, or even plastic surgery. A 24/7/365 pharmacy is always there when residents need it. A large store with every item residents may need or want bought in bulk and warehoused so it can be sold to residents at cost. Residents would also enjoy heated underground parking with 440 volt electrical outlets for biodiesel/electric hybrids. The state-of-the-art security will be the latest, and greatest available. Also available to residents could be furnished guest suites and party rooms. For entertainment, there could be a brew and view theater with microbrews and a traditional menu where residents could go and watch classic films. There could also be a traditional movie theater, and an IMAX theater where residents could watch the latest, greatest new releases with the best picture and sound quality ever. A Hollywood Blockbuster, a new animated film, or even a trip down the Amazon in 3D. Every building would have a Pre K-8 Academy where kids could take the elevator or the escalator to school instead of having thousands of school buses polluting the cities. There could be biodiesel/electric hybrid buses to take the high school children to and from the National Academy (talked about in Chapter 6) on the weekends. In addition, there could be retail and office space on-site.

The buildings eco-friendly design could keep residents utilities bill minimal. An air filtration system could filter, oxygenate, ionize, and even scent the air. A water filtration system could purify all incoming water. Boiling water taps and space saving/energy efficient appliances could make a nice addition. There could be a space saving washer and dryer in each unit, and then larger ones down the hall, for comforters and large loads, in the laundry rooms on each floor. Each floor could also have recycling chutes for paper, cardboard, glass, aluminum, and plastic.

Exterior amenities could include: a nine hole golf course, an amusement park, a hobby farm with horseback riding, apple, fruit, and nut orchards, a vineyard and winery, soccer, baseball, and other sports facilities, a small petting zoo, a community garden, small nature parks, an aquarium, an aviary with all types of birds, an arboretum and tree farm, a conservatory, and the possibilities are endless. Each building would have its own amenities, and the buildings would be linked by moving sidewalks, skyways, and monorails so residents of other condos can use all the amenities from all the buildings. All of this, and these mass produced condos would be cheaper, and last far longer, than their "one of a kind" counterparts.

For example, a Nonprofit Org designs and constructs the same condominium complex thousands of times. The more units they sell, the cheaper the individual units become. There could be 3 bedroom, 2 bathroom units in condominium complexes with all of the amenities, all connected by monorails. They could sell for a fraction of what people are paying now, and they could be constructed with the best materials by the best contractors and designed to last for over a century. Every part could be mass produced and prefabricated. Recycled materials could be used where possible, such as papercrete walls made from recycled paper and rubber floors in high traffic areas made from recycled automobile tires. The buildings would be built to last centuries, and every part that may need to be replaced in the future could be warehoused, cutting maintenance costs as well as construction costs.

Every building is the same basic design which saves billions on design costs for thousands of condominiums. Every part is mass produced and prefabricated saving billions. Every building is built by the same general and subcontractors keeping labor costs low and again saving billions. The final product is the worlds most advanced "self-contained city" with thousands of 3 bedroom 2 bathroom condominiums in buildings with every possible amenity. Every building would strive for carbon neutrality with photovoltaic solar panels, solar hot water, and even wind turbines. Most buildings could be built in cities and suburbs and connected to the rest of the city via moving sidewalks, tunnels, monorails, light rails, or biodiesel/electric hybrid buses. Buildings located in rural areas can be connected via high-speed maglev bullet trains to the nearest metropolitan areas and airports. Each building could have its own fleet of biodiesel/electric hybrid sport utility wagon taxis as well as hybrid shuttle vans. Each condo could have secure, underground parking with 440V hot spots and biodiesel fueling stations, so residents could charge up and fill up cheaply at home.

Cookie Cutter Town Homes and Tract Homes

These could be for people that want their own home with a yard, and some space between them and their neighbors, who do not want to live in a condo or self contained city. These homes would be the next generation town home and tract home. Their ultra-modern design could make them far superior to the ones being built today. They could strive for carbon neutrality using photo voltaic solar power, solar hot water, new insulation and windows, maybe even small wind turbines. They would be mass produced regionally and portions of them prefabricated where possible. The residents may even have the option of taking part in the construction of their new town home or tract home and putting in some "sweat equity". With materials and labor costs drastically reduced, a Nonprofit Org that specializes in finding people their dream home can sell the homes practically at cost. These town homes and tract homes could be more energy efficient, taking advantage of all of the newest technology in homebuilding. They could offer double glazed windows and insulation with high R values, smart meters, and solar hot water heaters and/or photovoltaic panels. All parts that would wear out over the decades would be warehoused. Any of the parts that a homeowner could possibly need for household repairs could be shipped the same day from a regionally located warehouse, making maintenance a cinch.

Cookie Cutter Self Contained Cities

In response to urban sprawl, it could be better to build up than build out. These Self Contained Cities would be similar to the cookie cutter condos, but much more immense in size and scope. They could be constructed later this century in response to the depletion of oil reserves and natural gas reserves. They could be a fully functioning city all enclosed in one building or series of buildings interconnected. They could produce all of their own energy with wind and solar power, and there could be solar hot water as well. They could have many of the same interior and exterior amenities that the cookie cutter condos have, but they would be massive in size, big enough to have thousands of units and house tens of thousands of people. The residents would rarely have to leave the Self Contained City in their lifetime, everything they could every possibly need is for sale at cost on-site. Maglev bullet trains would connect the cities to each other as well as to, other metropolitan areas, airports, sporting venues, and anywhere else residents may want to go.

Most of the amenities would be the same in every one of the thousands of Self Contained Cities in existence. The heated indoor and outdoor pool with water slides, as well as the sauna and eucalyptus steam room, and the ultimate fitness center with elliptical machines that generate electricity when in use. Also standard at every Self Contained City could be an international food court that delivers to any unit within minutes. This could include a micro-brew pub that delivers, combined with a small theater for stage and screen productions, where people can have a meal, and an adult beverage, while watching a movie, documentary or even a play. For evening entertainment, there could be a Studio 55 nightclub. There could also be a fleet of exotic cars, trucks, motorcycles, even yachts, sailboats, jets, jet skis, and other "toys" (all running on biodiesel) that residents can rent inexpensively. Each City would have a small airstrip and hangers. There would also be a biodiesel production facility that would make enough biodiesel to power all of the thousands of vehicles on-site. Residents would rarely need to drive, but there would be a fleet of large trucks running on biodiesel, as well as a fleet of biodiesel/electric hybrid SUV's and Shuttle Van Taxis that could take residents wherever, whenever.

Every Self Contained City would have its own daycare and pre-K-8 Academy. Kids could take the elevator to school. There would be thousands of jobs on-site for residents and their teen children. The Self Contained City would have to be as self sufficient as possible because much of what residents need comes in on trucks running on biodiesel or on the maglev trains.

These Self Contained Cities could practice self-sufficiency techniques such as vertical farming and hydroponics with hothouses to grow just about anything, except grains, which would be grown at the mechanized farms nearby. Self Contained Cities are typically near rural areas so they are usually surrounded by farms and ranches. They could have their own food processing facilities onsite or nearby. There could also be a collection of massive wind turbines as well as a multitude of solar arrays on the roof and in the surrounding area to help meet the city's energy requirements. The city's grey water can be treated and pumped back in to flush the two-stage toilets. All the blackwater could be combined with all of the food waste, and fed to red worms in a giant bin that vermicomposts everything, which produces worm castings, which are the best organic fertilizer. There could also be resomation on-site, so every time someone dies, their remains go into the fertilizer mixture. The bones do not resomate so they can be ground up and given to the family of the deceased. Sorry, that is a little morbid, but it could soon be a more popular option than cremation or burial.

There could also be an indoor mall with everything for sale at cost; there could be a farmers market with produce from local farmers; there could be indoor/outdoor sidewalk cafes, bakeries, ice cream parlors with dozens of flavors, where a person can create their own flavor. Residents will be able to pick from thousands of shops, restaurants, entertainment venues, parks, open spaces, there should be something for everyone.

Cookie Cutter Retirement Villas

Many factors could make it possible for people to live longer, healthier, more active lives. If the typical couple is being paired off with the national Matchmaker Program and having two children in their 20's and 30's, they could be sending their children off to the National Academy when they are in their 40's and 50's. They would probably want to stay put while the kids are at the academy, so the kids have someone and somewhere to come home to on weekends and holidays. Once their children have started their National Service, they could officially be out of the nest, freeing the parents up to retire. They could be 40-55 years old with a probable life expectancy of 80 or older. Generation 1 could have had better careers and made more money than people in previous generations. They could have also gotten better deals on everything they bought, saving them a bundle of money. Consequently, they would be retiring younger with more money than the historical average.

These cookie cutter Retirement Villas have everything retirees aged 40-100+ could ever possibly need or want sold to them at cost, or it could even be covered by insurance, and be free to the retiree. The list of amenities would vary based on locations, and market research, but every Retirement Villa could have many of the same amenities. Including, but not limited to: 24 hour buffet, day spa with daily massages, daily maid service, indoor and out door pools and hot tubs, saunas and eucalyptus steam rooms, 24hour health, dental, and vision clinics (retirees can get cosmetic surgery, cosmetic dentistry, laser eye surgery, etc.), and a 24/7/365 pharmacy. As a bronze, silver, gold, or platinum member, the retirees could have the option of staying at any of the retirement villas world wide. It could be like spending the rest of their life at a timeshare.

Many of these villas could be located in foreign nations and exotic locations with several interesting sites to see and plenty of opportunities for ecotourism. Members can take advantage of discounted airfare to get there. Based on what level membership they purchased they can use some or all of what the villas have to offer. Just about everything could be all-inclusive. Any other products or services could be at cost. The amenities would be similar to those a person would find on a cruise or at and all-inclusive resort: golf courses, water sports, casinos perhaps, scuba diving where possible, and the list is endless.

The goal would be to give more people than ever before the opportunity to retire early, and go enjoy themselves. These would be affordable, eco-friendly, mass produced, retirement villas. The Grandparents could do video chat with the grandkids or even have them come and stay in one of the guest suites for a week or two.

Cookie Cutter International Cities

No International City currently exists yet, but there could be hundreds of these cities on the outskirts of major international cities. They could cater to both city dwellers and people in rural areas. Every International City would be virtually the same, some might be larger than others, but they all have the basic core elements. Every part that goes into them is mass produced by the thousands saving millions on materials costs. By using the same general contractor to build every one of them, they would greatly reduce labor costs as well. The result could be a miniature version of a city with everything a person could possibly need bought in bulk and stored on-site.

The International City could consist of a landing strip and hanger for cargo planes that run on biodiesel, and deliver supplies all day. A fleet of 18 wheelers all running on biodiesel. A fleet of SUVs that are electric/biodiesel and can pull trailers (they might haul farm equipment on a trailer to a nearby farm), as well as hybrid pick-up trucks. The International Cities would produce all of their own biodiesel from algae pools on-site. The buildings would all be the same shell. Some would be partially earth bermed, and would have a sub level that could have tunnels connecting it to other buildings.

There would be massive warehouses, each the same on the outside, but configured differently on the inside. One could house every type of farm equipment, either electric or fueled with biodiesel (made on-site).

Other warehouses would have bulk supplies of dry goods. One of the mass produced warehouses would be configured as a store that would carry everything possible bought in bulk and sold at cost. There could also be one that has a refrigerated section. They could also have a fleet of electric forklifts that can move cargo around quickly (e.g. pallets of powdered milk from a warehouse to the kitchen). These warehouses could eventually expand to house everything the people in the surrounding region need. Water, food, medicine, building materials, farming equipment and tools, solar panels, wind turbines, and much more. In addition, there would be a fleet of trucks running on biodiesel that could deliver a load anywhere in their region the same day. They would also have every piece of farm equipment trailored and ready to be delivered to surrounding farms. What used to take weeks months, or even years, could now be done in a few days. They would be prepared for anything: war, revolution, a disease outbreak, famines, natural disasters, overpopulation, anything.

When people from the nearest metro area or the surrounding rural villages come to stay for a few days or longer, they would stay in the basic accommodations which could consist of a shelter with individual sleeping rooms, some with multiple beds like a hostel, each with a bathroom on each floor. There could also be hotel like accommodations for residents and visitors. Everyone who comes can all take advantage of the 24 hour buffet, for many this could be the best that they have eaten in their life. In addition, there could be a gigantic state-of-the-art high capacity hospital with all of the latest, greatest equipment, and many young doctors and nurses who are fulfilling their international service requirement or doing their residency. They would primarily be administering birth control to women and immunizations to children. They would be able to treat thousands of women and children per day at the larger cities.

All of the buildings in every city are basically the same and can be added to easily in the future by attaching another building. The hospital may need to expand to deal with a regional outbreak of some virus, the cafeteria may need to expand to feed refugees camped out in tents nearby.

There could also be a school with classes for people of all ages, as well as tutors to work with them. Everyone would be registered and tested with the results being saved in a database and sold to various companies for research purposes. The money could be used to help pay for the facilities. They may even have the option of participating in a medical research study, where they would try an investigational drug for the first time on humans, in exchange for their all inclusive stay. The school would also train adults in fields such as agriculture, as well as have courses on parenting and classes for children.

The typical scenario could be a fleet of biodiesel buses going in different directions picking people up at various stops, and bringing primarily women and children back to the International City. They get registered on the bus by a person with something like a palm pilot. If they are new, they establish an account. This gets them access to all of the facilities at the International City. If they are able to stay and find a job on-site, they could be paid with products and services. All food, temporary housing, and healthcare services are free. Upon arrival, they could be given a room in an enormous facility, down the hall they could have a modern bathroom with shower stalls where they can get cleaned up. They could then take a short walk over to the massive dining hall and eat at the buffet. Once they have finished eating they can make their way to the air conditioned, high capacity hospital where they can wait in comfortable, air conditioned waiting rooms with playrooms for the children. The women could get their birth control implant and the children their immunizations. All other medical issues could also be addressed at this time. Once finished at the hospital, they could go to the air conditioned school and take a class or two on the computer, use the Internet, watch some instructional videos, or do something educational and scholastic. By then, they may be hungry again and want to take another trip to the buffet. They might want to go for a swim first in the indoor/outdoor pool with a waterslide for the kids and some hot tubs for the adults. There could also be a sauna (probably cooler than it is outside in some locations) and a eucalyptus steam room. There could be a larger building with an auditorium which could seat thousands of people. It could be used to show movies or educational videos. The air conditioned auditorium could be used to teach classes and hold seminars during the day. At night, it could double as a small movie theater where residents and guests could bring their children for a movie before 'lights out'. The entire facility could be powered with wind and solar power and could exist off grid indefinitely.

There could be hundreds of online and video presentations that adults and children can watch while they stay for a few days. Each time they come they could be able to increase their knowledge base. They could build a mental toolbox full of useful information on parenting, sanitation, disease prevention, agriculture, or simply how to read and write their language of choice. The instruction could be done in a video speaking their language, they would not need to know how to read and write, they would simply have to listen and use a touch screen to pick the right answer. There could also be game-like, educational, interactive software programs for children as young as 3. All of these courses could be specially designed for adults and children in their area or region, to provide useful knowledge they can use to support themselves and live healthier lives. If they are coming every year to three years over a 20 year period and taking 2-4 courses during the time they are there, the adults and children could take anywhere from 15-75 courses over the 20 year period. Some of these people have never taken a course in anything in their lives. Dads could be encouraged to come along each trip as well. If mom, dad, and the two children take different courses each time, they could have collectively taken 60-300 courses between them. There could be millions of people getting free education.

Some of the goals of these facilities would be to get every woman birth control by giving her an implant every 3 years. When a woman finds a life partner she can take some parenting classes at the International City, and achieve a parenting license. She could also get some free gifts and financial assistance to help her be the best parent she can be. After she has the child, she could go back on birth control or possibly get surgically sterilized at the medical facility.

There could be a specially designed facility for the elderly and the infirm. It could be able to accommodate many of the elderly patients in the region allowing them some medical treatment before they expire. There could be the option of euthanasia for people who have been there for awhile and whose condition is fatal and untreatable. They could also have the option of spending one last visit with their family before they are euthanized. Their bodies can then be resomated and turned into fertilizer for the surrounding farms.

There could also be a children's hospital on-site that would take in sick children from the adjacent cities and the surrounding region. Along with the children's hospital, there could be a colossal orphanage on-site that would house every orphan in the region. The children could be raised to the ages of 16 to 18 and educated and trained to live a productive life in a nearby city or village.

There could also be the regions largest boarding school on-site. The cost per pupil would be minimal and could be paid by the pupils family (who may be able to work it off), paid by a grant or scholarship, or paid for with a loan that the student could pay back by working at the facility a certain number of hours per school year.

Many adults and even some children could have the opportunity to apply for one of thousands of jobs in the monumental complex. Many children from the orphanage could start working when they are 15, and be prepared mentally, physically, and financially for the new society they are about to become a member of.

There could also be a University, with thousands of students living on-site in the International City in student housing. They could train for careers that could help their city and nation. Graduates could have the option of working and living on-site at the International City.

Everyone who comes to the facility is thoroughly documented to help compile statistics and get an accurate census. Residents and guests could have the opportunity to participate in medical research trials, as well as have their stories featured in one of many documentaries that could be made in their region. They could get paid with products and services for their participation. Every child could be given a world ID number that they could have the rest of their life. This way every child could be registered and can use their ID number for obtaining assistance, going to school, voting, and many other important uses.

The facilities could also have emergency response units that respond to natural disasters and other extreme situations such as wars, revolutions, disease outbreaks, famines, and anything else that may occur. They could have water, food, medical supplies, tents and anything else they need ready to go on a moments notice. There could also be a military type barracks, and training facility, for a Global Peace Keeping Force that can have wheels up in 15 minutes, and boots on the ground within hours. GPKF Paratroopers are trained to be first on-site day or night. The rest of the force follows their lead as they work in unison with all of the other soldiers coming in from other regions. They would be capable of flooding any area in the world with thousands of troops within a day or two. Re-supplying them could be much easier, due to the fact that they have these new regionally located International Cities. The Peace Keepers could also be charged with securing the facility and operating checkpoints at the International Cities when they are not deployed. They may also go on peace keeping missions, and work on security for the International Cities and the surrounding regions. They could eventually be the strongest force in each region they are in. There would no longer be any need for any smaller nations to have a military.

Each city could have its own airstrips and hangars full of military aircraft, as well as cargo planes with their internationally known logo on the side. Everyone on earth could recognize the logo when they see it.

It could be on every thing in the facility. The entire facility is re-supplied by goods being brought in on the cargo planes and being trucked in with biodiesel/electric trucks also adorned with the memorable logo. They could stockpile everything the facility would need to operate for months at a time without needing another shipment. Fruit and vegetable juice concentrates, powdered, fortified milk (with strawberry and chocolate for the kids). Dehydrated meats, as well as, peanut butter, and other protein rich foods. Plus, water purification kits with iodine, or the equivalent. The International Cities could have their own generic brand of everything produced right within the cities or specifically for the cities. The products would all be sold at cost, or given away free. Every single product would have the logo on it.

There could be massive farms and pastureland adjacent to the International Cities that could supply much of the food served on-site. Very little would have to be brought in. There could also be an industrial city within the International City that focuses on manufacturing goods and anything else the region may need. This would create thousands of opportunities for people in the region to live and work on-site, as well as have their kids go to school on-site.

The International Cities would also host anyone coming to visit the region including, missionaries, celebrities, Churches, Charities, scientists, researchers, documentary film makers, Peace Corp Volunteers, and myriad other people that would want to visit the region for personal or professional reasons. The International City would help outfit and supply them with reliable transportation and anything else they need including the best guides in the region. They could continue to re-supply them for the duration of their stay. This would offer visitors a home away from home and the opportunity to see the region hassle free and have a nice place to come "home" to until they depart the region.

They would also work closely with their host nations in the region they are in. They would help build their nations with experts from around the globe. They could offer courses, lectures, seminars, training for civil servants, and other beneficial services. They could also have a specially trained staff that helps educate voters in the surrounding areas and helps nations hold free, peaceful, national elections. If a civil war does break out, they could have the means to shut it down in a shorter period of time than any other group on earth.

The Pilot Project could begin as soon as 2020. An International City could be built. Once constructed, the new International City and the surrounding area would be able to offer a haven for a million plus refugees. The International City could have supplies either flown in with cargo planes running on biodiesel or trucked in with trucks running on biodiesel. The International City would have the worlds largest biodiesel storage facilities. They would produce their own biodiesel on-site from algae. They would have specially designed tanker trucks (running on biodiesel) that would deliver the biodiesel to filling stations in the region.

A fleet of all terrain double-decker, air conditioned buses with rugged suspensions and rugged terrain tires would pick up wave after wave of people and bring them in for processing. The buses would have the trademark color and logo. In "hot zones", they could have military escorts from the Global Peace Keeping Forces stationed at the International Cities. Upon arrival, local citizens could be assigned a number. The sick and injured could be taken immediately. The rest of the people would get registered and then they could proceed to the dining hall or the hospital. The children would be given immunizations, the mothers would get a birth control implant good for 3 years. Once they are done at the hospital, they will be assigned a room or a tent. They will be able to use the outdoor pool with waterslides for the kids, while the adults sit in the hot tubs. They could be encouraged to use the pool, shower facilities, and dining hall as often as they like. If they need further medical attention they can return to the hospital as well. They will be given a biodegradable backpack full of items they and their families need, such as toiletries, candy and toys for the kids, medicines, mosquito nets and much more. They could also be given a gift card good at the general store so they can buy any other items they need. Every effort would be made to make their stay as comfortable as possible. They could go to the computer lab and take some courses, they could go watch movies and documentaries in the auditorium with other families, or any number of activities depending on the situation.

The goal of the International Cities could be to make sure every child in the region is getting their basic needs met; water, food, healthcare, shelter, and education. They could also try to provide stability in the region by resolving conflicts, they could also help facilitate elections in their host nations or other nearby nations. Over the decades, there should be less human suffering, less extreme poverty, fewer unwanted pregnancies, less civil unrest, less war and violence, and no child should die of dehydration, starvation, or a preventable disease.

Summary

Cookie cutter construction and mass production is going to house more people more affordably, more efficiently, and offer them more amenities, than ever before in history. For the first time, billions of people will be able to own property and leave it to their children. Their children could have a better education and more career opportunities, allowing them to trade up to better housing. The perfectly good unit they sell is some young couples dream condo. Gradually, over a few generations, everybody's housing situations will improve dramatically. This could be revolutionary.

6

A Child Miseducated is a Child Lost[21]

THIS WAS YET another brilliant JFK quote from the end of his State of the Union address in January, 1962. In 1965, there was the elementary and Secondary School Act as part of President Johnson's Great Society legislation. There have been 50 years of innovation in education. If experience is the best teacher, the United States could take 50 years worth of empirical data, combined with other factors such as the most diverse population in the world, and use it to create ultra-modern "super schools". Students from every possible background could come together at these new National Academies and not just learn academically, but learn to work together, play together, win together, lose together, and learn from their mistakes and be the best and brightest generation of young adults ever, for their age.

Once the students have completed their 4 years of high school at these new National Academies, at 18 they could go on to do National Service. This National Service could consist of a training session that would be the same for every young man and woman. There would be both a mental and physical conditioning and training regimen that every

---

21   http://www.brainyquote.com/quotes/quotes/j/johnfkenn114943.html

recent graduate would adhere to everyday. After they graduate from their "boot camp", they would go to their individual advanced training for their particular National Service assignment. They should be healthy and in the best shape of their lives. Many of them would be traveling to different cities and nations. The entire 2 years of National Service can be used for college credit. Students would also get a living stipend as well as grants, scholarships, and money for school.

If the Fast Track Program has done its job right, the young man or woman should be going to the school that best suits them. They could also take the career path that is right for them. They could use the Match Maker Program to find a life mate and from there they could go on to take parenting classes, obtain a parenting license, get married and have children of their own. They could meet the parenting standard, and before they know it, their teenage son or daughter could be attending an academy like they did.

National Academy

Future children could start pre-kindergarten – a quarter day program preparing 2-4 year olds for the "rigors" of life as a kindergartner. From ages 5-13, every child could attend a full day, fully integrated, multicultural grade school and National Academy preparatory school. At the age of 13, every child could enter the National Academy.

The vast majority of the population could be living in cookie cutter condominiums with Pre-K through 8th grade academies right on-site. The children could take the elevator to school instead of a school bus. For those students who live in the new tract homes and town homes, the new mobile home parks, and other communities, they could take buses running on biodiesel to a local Pre-K through 8th grade elementary/junior high, possibly an old high school converted into a National Academy Preparatory Academy. All of these grade schools could compete in academic and athletic contests. Along with a parenting standard, there could also be a standardized curriculum and educational standard requiring each child to make sufficient progress to meet or exceed the standard. Students who are struggling to meet the standard could get the extra attention they need. It might just be a matter of using some interactive software that helps them in one or more particular subjects. The primary goal of these Pre-K through 8th grade schools could be to prepare students for the National Academy.

The children would have a full school year, with only a few breaks and holidays. Families could be encouraged to join one or more of the educational field trips offered during the breaks. The families and members of the community could take a very active role in the education and socialization of these children. Most children could have 8 great grandparents, retired in cookie cutter retirement villas whom they can video chat with, as well as 4 grandparents, who may live and work nearby in the surrounding community, or be in retirement villas themselves. Each child could have two parents who play an especially active role in their educational process.

Parents could have a shorter work week, and they could have at least three days off per week, giving them the opportunity to spend more quality time with their families. There could be field trips where the parents join their children as chaperones on short and long journeys to places of interest. If students are learning a second language, they may be eligible for a discounted vacation to another nation during their short breaks or vacations.

When the students graduate from junior high (grade 8) at about the age of 13, they should have an exceptionally well rounded education, and should be prepared for their educational experience at the National Academy. Typically, the National Academies could be regionally located in rural settings. These National Academies would be similar to a large college campus, where students 13 to 18 live on-site. These National Academies could have been designed by experts in every possible field drawing on 50 years of experience in the US Public and Private Schools.

Students could live in a dormitory type setting where they could share a room with one or more students, with the option of maybe getting a single room their junior and senior years, if they become a resident assistant. Most classes could be held in smaller classrooms with 10-20 students, but there may also be online courses and some classes may be held with hundreds of students in an auditorium. There could be giant sports complexes for every possible sport as well as facilities for every other possible extra-curricular activity imaginable. The drama department could have state of the art equipment for students to make their own Student TV station, and documentaries, for example. There could also be a music studio where aspiring artists from every genre can practice and record music. A fully equipped fitness center where students can watch their favorite program while they do 30 minutes on the elliptical trainer, while athletes train a little harder for their particular sport/s. There could be special emphasis on keeping every student at their ideal body weight, which may mean specific diets, and extra time in the fitness center. There would be health food restaurants with low calorie food that is filling, and tastes good. Also, the workout equipment would be fun to use, so kids who were putting on weight, could easily take it off. Obesity is becoming a bigger problem everyday. The kids at risk for obesity will have understanding counselors and dieticians who have dealt with the problem for decades.

The Academy could also feature an international food court where students can choose from dozens of restaurants to eat at (variety is the spice of life). There could be a large mall where everything is affordable for students on a budget. Each Academy could also have its own IMAX movie theater for educational trips to Alaska or the latest Hollywood blockbuster. There could be a military style ROTC training facility that can also be used for next generation paint ball and laser tag leagues. The possibilities are endless.

Every Academy, depending on the geographical location, would take one or more longer field trips to places of interest in the region. The film students could cover the entire trip, so that it can be shared with students at other academies in their IMAX theaters. This could make it seem as if they were on the field trip with them. An example might be, a regional Academy located in the east takes a 2 week spring or autumn field trip to civil war sites, and even participates in some reenactments. The film students document the whole excursion. Field trips at some of the western Academies might visit Alaska or Hawaii, documenting every part of the journey for students in the rest of the nation to see in their Academies IMAX style theater.

Every weekend the students can have a good time at one of the campuses parties or clubs. There could be a plethora of entertainment options from watching sports on the big screen to dee-jaying and dancing at a simulated nightclub with non-alcoholic energy drinks. Academy students may also want to make their own movies or jam with a band. The possibilities could be endless.

These academies could be mass produced and built to last, alumni could be coming to their great grandchildren's graduation 60 years after they've graduated.

Every school has its own clinic and every student gets free comprehensive health, dental, and vision, including birth control. There could be mandatory preventive health care courses students can complete online, in class, and in the auditorium.

There could be religious services for every possible religion, usually held on the weekend.

Every student will complete high school by age 19 so they can move on to their National Service commitment. If students are struggling to meet this requirement, they could have special tutors assigned to them. Young adults who are performing well in their academic pursuits, may be rewarded with a job tutoring other students who are struggling academically. This could be a good part time job for a student that is looking at going into education when they graduate. There could be an abundance of employment opportunities on-site at the National Academies for children 14 and older. Some students who are more advanced may have the option of graduating the National Academy at 17 and completing their National Service early.

There could be a profusion of foreign exchange students from every nation spending anywhere from 1 to 4 years at the National Academy.

The students graduating from the Academy should be the most advanced people their age in the world. They should have developed admiration for their nation, as well as a sense of noblesse oblige, a desire to go out and make a difference in the world. National Service will give them the skills they need to do just that.

One of the things they may chose to do to fulfill their mandatory National Service obligation is work at one of the new World Class Academies. They can help foreign students learn English as their primary or secondary language. They could also educate children and young adults on a variety of other topics.

Sidewalk cafes make a nice hangout before and after class. A fashion design center where students can create clothing for themselves and others such as screen printing and making t-shirts. Students can make their own music in the recording studio, they can have their own TV Station and do films and documentaries, the students can use the auto shop to pimp some rides, there could be a science fair every year with students working on their science projects, there could also be some interesting new physical education classes such as laser tag, rock climbing, and whatever is popular.

Fast Track Program

When the students are ready, the teacher will appear. Starting at age 4, the Fast Track Program begins guiding students through their academic career. It will have specially designed tests for every age and skill level. It may give students a battery of mental and physical aptitude tests as well as personality inventories and career guidance aptitude tests. The Fast Track Program tracks students from pre-K, until they have completed their academic career. With data from the Fast Track Program, they could be aided in selecting the right educational field to study, as well as, the best National Service option for them. Students may change their course of study, or their National Service option, until they are juniors and/or seniors, at which time they could begin taking electives that relate closely to their course of study, and their choice of future National Service commitments.

National Service

At the age of 18, in most cases, every student could have chosen his or her preferred option for their 2 year commitment of National Service. The military, the peace corps, and other Organizations may do campus recruiting via satellite in the auditorium, where they give an audio visual presentation and hold a questions and answers session afterwards.

This National Service requirement could be fulfilled in many ways. The recent National Academy graduates may have been in an ROTC program, in which case they would choose a branch of the military or some other national security or law enforcement position. Some of their options could be the Army, Navy, Air Force, Marines, Coast Guard, Border Patrol, or International Service as a U.N. Peace Keeper.

The US military could have millions of soldiers on active duty somewhere at home or abroad and millions more in the reserves. The US military could be the largest, best trained, best equipped military on earth.

Of course, the military is not for everybody, which is why there could be numerous other National Service options, such as the Peace Corp. The Peace Corp armed with millions of volunteers, and all of the equipment and supplies they need, could get so much accomplished, they might put themselves out of business. Millions of Peace Corp alumni could have Peace Corp license plates, and their own hangouts, similar to VFW's, where they could get together and tell stories about the toughest job they ever loved.

Another National Service option would be Americorp/Vista or something similar to it. Millions of Americorps volunteers could flood the major metropolitan areas and work on a variety of projects that would help build and shape the new America.

The other options could be to do missionary type work for a church, charity, Nonprofit Organization, or some similar form of national or international service. Millions of young men and women committed to making the world a better place volunteering in every corner of the earth would solve most international problems within a few generations.

After they have completed their two year national service commitment, every graduate will receive a two week paid vacation that will quickly become a perennial party period.

World Class International Academy

Every nation could agree upon a standard curriculum developed by a panel of leading experts from every subject. This core curriculum could be taught in traditional schools or they could go to their nearest World Class International Academy and get a more in depth study of the core curriculum as well as additional courses. It could be the first time in world history every child not only gets an education, but gets the same or similar education as every other child on every other continent. Every child could learn the same basic lessons as every other child in the world. Every student could learn English as a primary or secondary language. There could also be classes taught in their native language and classes designed specifically for their regional location. These Academies would be similar to an Academy in the US, or the UK. There could be thousands of these Academies worldwide. Each Academy could be a free standing structure that is mass produced and laid out the same as every other one.

These academies would be a good place for American National Academy graduates to do their National Service. It would also be an excellent opportunity for teachers at the Academies who would be drawn from a pool of the best local educators.

International Service

This could be the international equivalent of National Service. Every graduate from a World Class Academy could have the opportunity to do two years of International Service. They would receive educational funding they could use to study at an accredited University or school of any other kind.

Summary

Great minds tend to think alike and like minds tend to assimilate, but not all great minds assimilate. It seems like the citizens of the US can not agree on anything. However, there is one thing everyone should agree on, and that is that the US should be number one. The US is not going to fix itself, but with the accumulated, collective wisdom of millions of people from as many backgrounds, with as many histories, future generations are going to be the best and brightest the world has ever had to offer. These next generations will make this the greatest nation that ever existed. These future generations could be the ones who go out into the world armed with ideas that work. Whether they are in Americorps, the Peace Corps or the Marine Corps, they could be on the front lines, working together to build the greatest empire that ever existed.

Appendix A

THE JUXTAPOSITION OF the timelines shows the destructive path the US and the human race are on. The possibilities laid out in the alternative timeline can be a "to do list" for future generations, or they can be disregarded as impractical, improbable, even impossible. If it's believable, it's achievable. Where there's a will there's a way.

Current Course Timeline

2010-2025

- Millions of unplanned pregnancies nearly double the world's population
- Millions of children suffer and die every year from lack of potable water, malnutrition, preventable diseases, and other causes.
- Millions of adults die prematurely; millions more suffer unnecessarily.
- Most of the world lives on less than $1 a day.
- There continues to be wars, civil wars, revolutions, and armed conflicts, internationally
- There continues to be desertification taking over valuable cropland, rapidly advancing and negatively affecting billions of people.
- There continues to be massive deforestation of the tropics.

- Peak oil, peak natural gas, peak phosphorus, and peak soil result in higher oil, natural gas, and phosphorus prices.
- There is no way to buy new soil, and building soil could take decades, so most of the world would have little if any good soil. A true global pandemic.
- Carbon emissions continue to increase, especially with new coal fired electric plants being built and more drivers than ever imagined driving vehicles with gas combustible engines
- Women who are not mentally, physically, and financially ready continue to have multiple children in the US and the world.
- Children continue to get neglected and abused or worse, oftentimes by someone they knew and trusted.
- The crippling national debt of 14 trillion turns into 40 trillion, and is handed down to future generations.
- Over fishing has a long term ecological impact and results in the extinction of many fish species including tuna and cod.
- Big multinational corporations try to sell water to people who can barely afford it at ridiculously high prices.
- More kids hurt the nation than help it

2025-2050

- The world population could be over 10 billion with most of the recent additions in some of the poorest countries.
- Now 5 children are dying every second instead of 1 child dying every 5 seconds.
- The number of children who die every year could be in the tens of millions.
- Hundreds of millions of women who are not mentally, physically, and financially ready could continue to have multiple children
- The number of children who are dehydrated, malnourished, sick, dying, homeless, sold into slavery, and worse could rise dramatically with no possible solution.
- The number of people in extreme poverty could have increased dramatically with no possible solution.
- Wars, revolutions, plagues, famines, and natural disasters could rage on killing billions with no apparent end in sight.
- The world could be out of oil
- Desertification could have enveloped even more of the planet rendering the land permanently useless.

- Deforestation could have wiped out almost all of the tropical rainforests permanently.
- The US federal debt could have escalated to over 40 trillion with no realistic possibility of paying it off.

Appendix B

Alternative Course Timeline

2010-2025

- On 3-22-12, World Water Day, the Nonprofit Org (WWP) announces its new World Water Program and opens the first of thousands of desalination plants.
- A bill is introduced in the US Congress that requires all mothers to take a parenting class online and pass a readiness test if they are going to receive any government funding.
- Another bill is introduced that would encourage everyone under the age of 21 to do 2 or more years of National Service by offering them up to $50,000 in education grants.
- 18 year old young men and women will serve 2 years for 1 cause and make a commitment that lasts a lifetime.
- The US builds the first of several National Academies as a pilot program. Millions of 13 year olds take entrance exams and write essays about why they want to get in.
- A Nonprofit Organization begins making biodiesel from algae.
- The United States becomes the world's leading producer of biodiesel made from algae. Foreign orders are piling up
- This biodiesel is soon offered at most gas stations.

- The new World Car Sport Utility Wagon is unveiled. It is capable of getting over 100 miles to the gallon. It is a biodiesel/electric hybrid with a 4 or 6 cylinder diesel engine. The diesel engine runs on biodiesel and kicks in at 35 miles per hour and has a top speed up to 100 miles per hour. The World Car NPO pre-sells millions.
- The new Industrial Cities, create millions of jobs nationally and many more internationally.
- The worlds largest wind farm is constructed, stretching across 16 states and generating over half of the nations power
- The Government requires cleaner coal and oil power plants.
- The Government embarks on a 25 year plan to pay off the national debt.
- A Nonprofit Org constructs thousands of cookie-cutter condos with 3 bedroom 2 bathroom units for sale cheaper than rent. To combat urban sprawl, cities are trying to build up not out.
- A Nonprofit Org starts building new carbon neutral prefabricated mobile homes and placing them in new mobile home parks with all the amenities.
- Cookie-cutter group homes are being mass produced.
- The Government puts in high-speed maglev rail network connecting every major metropolitan area.
- Jets begin running on a mixture of jet fuel, ethanol, and biodiesel as engineers design planes that could run entirely on biodiesel.
- Most truck stops carry biodiesel cheaper than regular diesel so most shipping companies require their drivers to use biodiesel.
- Every school and city bus begins running on biodiesel and electric power.
- The government offers a tax credit for any home or building that uses solar electricity, solar hot water, or wind power or any combination of the three.
- The US declares a moratorium on building new coal plants and requires all existing coal fired electric plants to upgrade and start using new "clean coal" technology or shut down. Clean Coal plants are given until 2050.
- The energy companies offer incentives for people who buy electric appliances such as ovens/ranges, clothes dryers, hot water heaters and furnaces, instead of ones that require natural gas.
- Wind & solar energy make electricity cheaper than natural gas.
- Nonprofit Org begins to put an end to child abuse of every kind.

- A Nonprofit Org begins to offer cheap or free birth control to anyone who wants it. Women and men who come in get a gift card or free meal at a local restaurant.
- Fast Track Program is required for every student age 4-18
- Matchmaker Program becomes the best online service of its kind.
- Documentary channel is offered in HD on every cable and dish network.
- The government offers affordable healthcare to every citizen
- New International Health Clinics start popping up in many cities around the world with locations in the thousands
- Everything that ran on gasoline is converted to run on biodiesel. From heavy equipment to small engines (motorcycles, lawnmowers, boat engines, etc.)
- Nonprofit fertilizer making facilities are mass produced and several are built near every major city on earth. These facilities have the cities grey and black water channeled to them where it is treated and used as "humanure" Organic fertilizer.
- In addition, all of the food waste from every city is brought in and vermicomposted (fed to red worms) and turned into worm castings to be used as fertilizer.
- Most people choose to be resomated
- This fertilizer combined with massive amounts of irrigation water from the new desal plants begins to reverse the desertification, turning desert into farms, pastures, orchards, vineyards, etc.
- Many International Cities are built on the outskirts of many overcrowded, impoverished cities.
- Global Peacekeepers begin training for missions on every continent at International Cities on every continent.
- Mass produced desal plants are being strategically placed all over the globe.
- Food production reaches an all time high as a result of new agricultural practices and an abundance of water.
- Generation 1 is starting to be born to licensed parents
- NASCAR has its first ever race where every car is running on biodiesel
- All petroleum and petroleum based products become obsolete in the US and replaced with biodiesel and other substitutes.
- North American soil is gradually being rebuilt with a goal of being chemical free by 2020. Mostly Organic herbicides, pesticides, fungicides, and fertilizers are being used.

- 2020 is dubbed the year of the woman and both presidential candidates are women who decide to run on a bipartisan ticket
- The 20/20 Vision is released on the Internet in every language. It outlines the best course of action for humans to take in the coming decades.

2025-2050

- For the first time ever the entire human race is united
- The Nonprofit World Water Program has just built its thousandth mega desal plant
- There is an abundance of water for billions of people who had none 10 years ago.
- There is an abundance of food for everyone, the worms eat better than humans used to.
- A Nonprofit Org is manufacturing a new gas grill that runs on biodiesel
- There are thousands of industrial cities creating millions of jobs directly and indirectly.
- World Cars are nearing the 2 billion sold mark.
- The world population has not risen as much, particularly in developing nations where New Cities are being built and offering free birth control and immunizations
- All children born are planned for and have 2 licensed parents.
- Every child's basic needs are met
- The US becomes the world's largest exporter of biodiesel
- The ocean levels are barely rising
- Water pipelines bring water to every part of the planet that needs it
- There is over a ten year supply of food stockpiled for every human.
- Every child has health, dental, and vision coverage from conception to death
- Every human lives in above adequate shelter, most people have their own room
- Every student knows English as a primary or secondary language
- Every US citizen has used Fast Track from 4-18.
- Every child is born to licensed parents, attends the National Academy, does their National Service, gets paired off with Matchmaker, gets married, takes parenting classes . . .
- Every US citizen is retired by 50 and is collecting benefits and living in a retirement villa

- Every person chooses when they want to die and then has their body resomated
- Desertification is not only stopped, it is reversed and humans start farming every arable acre Organically with a new kind of fertilizer made up of worm castings, humanure, and resomated dead bodies
- Every vehicle is an electric/biodiesel hybrid
- Every city is full of cookie cutter condos
- Every suburban and rural area has new mobile home parks, town homes, and tract homes
- Cookie cutter shelters and group homes have ended homelessness and replaced the tin roof shanties in the slums in and around most major cities
- Deforestation has stopped and new trees are being planted.
- Every person has everything they need and most of what they want
- The environment is repaired
- The human race lives happily ever after.

> "Three things will last forever–faith, hope, and love–and the greatest of these is love."–**Saint Paul**[22]

---

[22]   Bible–New Living Translation–1 Corinthians 13:13, (n.d.). retrieved from http://bible.cc/1_corinthians/13-13.htm

Appendix C

Carbon Free by 2050

A GREEN PEACE article from the New York Times in 1990 read, "It wasn't the *Exxon Valdez's* captains driving that caused the oil spill. It was yours."

If the next page had been a full page ad for an automobile that used no oil, gas, or fossil fuels of any kind, priced comparably to the vehicle the reader drives with the same performance as the readers vehicle, many readers may have traded their vehicle with the gas combustible engine in for this new CO_2 free car. It is not that vehicle owners and operators want to pollute the air or cause oil spills, it is that they do not have a choice. Their only "eco-friendly" option is an electric hybrid which still uses oil and gas.

In the case of automobiles, trucks, buses, planes, and any other form of transport that runs on fuel, they could soon be running on biodiesel. Originally, biodiesel was made from things such as vegetable or soy oil. It would have taken up millions of acres of prime farmland to grow enough soy or other crops to make biodiesel. Ethanol made from corn ran into the same problem, the amount of time and money spent extracting the ethanol did not really do much to help the environment. Additionally, ethanol production was taking up valuable cropland and using corn that could have been used to feed humans or livestock to make ethanol for limousines and hummers. However, recent research has proven that biodiesel can be extracted from certain kinds of algae. Biodiesel made from corn could yield about 15 gallons of oil per acre, per year, whereas algae may produce up to 15,000 gallons of biodiesel in that same acre, but unlike corn or soybeans, algae do not need good soil, perfect temperatures, constant irrigating and fertilizing, tilling and planting. Algae is much easier to transport and process as well. Enough biodiesel rich algae could be grown on about 30-40 million acres to completely replace gas, plus these algae facilities can be placed on land that is not suitable for agriculture, so they would not take up any valuable farmland.

Ethanol currently uses about 16 million acres of valuable cropland, and does not even replace gasoline, it is just an additive that can replace about 5%-25% of a gallon of gasoline. Unlike ethanol, biodiesel completely replaces such things as gas, oil, and jet fuel.

The biodiesel facilities could be placed next to coal, oil, and natural gas fired electric plants and the algae can be used to sequester the carbon these fossil fuel burning plants release and turn it into biodiesel. Biodiesel production facilities could also be located next to sewage treatment plants where the algae could feed on the nitrogen and phosphate rich waste water and turn it into biodiesel. Big oil companies are investing huge sums of money in the research and development of producing biodiesel from algae, similar to when the ethanol industry was about to take off. There is already some gas stations and truck stops offering biodiesel. The prices could be significantly less than refined gasoline which requires a much more extensive and expensive process to produce. Most large trucks have diesel engines, soon all cars could too. This new biodiesel could work in any diesel engine without any modifications. Future diesel engines could be specifically designed to run solely on biodiesel. Biofuels could be made and used everywhere on earth by the end of the century. This is revolutionary!

A gallon of gasoline is assumed to produce 8.8 kilograms (or 19.4 pounds) of CO_2.[23] A gallon of biodiesel produces *none*. Bio fuels could reduce auto emissions, but auto emissions are only about 15% of the world's CO_2 output (burning oil is about 45%, coal 35%, and natural

---

[23] 2010, The US EPA: *Emission Facts: Greenhouse Gas Emissions From A Typical Passenger Vehicle* retrieved from *http://www.epa.gov/oms/climate/420f05004. htm*

gas 25%) and CO_2 only makes up 75% of the world's greenhouse gas emissions with the other 25 % being made up of methane, roughly 15%, and nitrous oxide and fluorocarbons making up about 5% each. So, even if everyone walked to work every day, it would not do much to reduce greenhouse gases, but if drivers were offered an alternative such as a biodiesel/electric hybrid that performed as good or better, priced as cheap or cheaper than what they are driving today, they would almost certainly buy it.

There could even be biodiesel/electric hybrids. These diesel engines should last longer typically than those that ran on gasoline, consequently the cost to operate vehicles could be less than it used to be. All automobiles could be cheaper to produce, last longer, sell for less, and the biodiesel they use could be much cheaper than gasoline was. There could be cheaper cars that run on cheaper fuel that does not harm the environment making it more affordable for more people to drive, particularly in other nations like China and India who could add a billion new drivers. The only down side is, there would be more traffic congestion.

A new type of hybrid could emerge that could use biodiesel and electricity to power it. The electric engine would propel it for speeds up to 35 miles per hour. It could have a small diesel generator onboard that could help recharge the battery. It could also use regenerative braking to recharge the battery pack. By the time they reach the market, most nations could have converted to wind and solar power so when people plug their car in at night for a 4 hour charge, the electricity used could be carbon free. These biodiesel/electric hybrids would also have a secondary 4,6, or 8 cylinder diesel engine that could run on biodiesel. Since electric and biodiesel engines last longer and are easier to maintain, they would not only be a better choice for the environment, they could be a better value than their gas powered predecessors. Also, biodiesel and electricity could be cheaper than they are now, making them much cheaper to operate. These automobiles could go thousands of miles between trips to the biodiesel station. Cars, trucks, and SUV's would have plenty of passing and towing power. These vehicles could easily get over 100 miles to the gallon and if recharged every night would have an almost unlimited range. If the typical driver drives an average of 35 miles per day they would rarely if ever use the diesel engine. There could be a fleet of vehicles; compact cars, sedans, sports cars, light and heavy duty pickups, SUV's, Sport Utility Wagons, Mini-Vans, Passenger Vans, even motorcycles, small engines (lawn mowers, boat motors, snow blowers) all running on electricity and biodiesel. Gas could be a thing of the past.

This new line of automobiles and smaller engines (snowmobiles, jet skis, ATV's (All Terrain Vehicles)) could also be designed and built in the US creating much needed career opportunities. The production facilities could be part of the new Industrial Cities. Employees who work in one of the many manufacturing facilities could live on-site in employee housing. While they will not make as much in salary as auto workers today receive, they could get a comprehensive benefits package including education benefits for their children and retirement benefits for themselves.

There could also be massive biodiesel production facilities near existing power plants on the outskirts of every major metropolitan area. Tankers trucks running on biodiesel themselves could deliver the biodiesel to the stations. Since it could be cheaper to manufacture, process, and ship to its final destination than regular diesel gasoline, it should cost significantly less at the pump. Eventually, they could start carrying biodiesel at every gas station and prices would come down even further as a result of the sales volume increase. Unlike fossil fuels, it is 100% renewable.

Eventually, these biodiesel/electric hybrids would become more affordable and everyone in the world would drive one, completely eliminating all CO_2 emissions from automobiles, trucks, buses, motorcycles, and other gas combustible engines. Gas stations would become biodiesel stations that carry two grades of biodiesel, regular, and premium.

This could completely eliminate the need for oil and gasoline powered vehicles. This could mean complete oil independence thus averting the *peak oil* catastrophe. By the time these vehicles do hit the market, America could have converted to wind energy with giant wind farms in several states connected to a new power grid that meets every American's energy needs without any fossil fuels (coal, oil, natural gas), the nation can also switch from natural gas appliances to what could be new cheaper electric appliances thus averting the *peak natural gas* tragedy. Americans could pay much less for electricity than they do now because wind farms are cheap, easy to build and maintain and could last longer than all other sources of electricity production. The little bit of electricity needed to charge these electric hybrids if they even need to be recharged (some could be recharged while driving and braking) would be minimal. These cars would pay for themselves in fuel saving over a 5, 7, or 10+ year timeframe.

For high traffic routes such as large public universities, airports, malls, sports venues, and crowded business districts, there could be light rail and/or monorail connecting hotels and convention centers to the airport for example. With the abundance of wind energy that we could see by as early as 2020 or 2030, light rails and monorails could be a carbon free option for public transportation. There could also be diesel/electric hybrid buses, green taxis, and shuttles, and any others that would be able to get people from point A to point B with no carbon emissions. People coming in for conventions, for example, could rent a hybrid for the duration of their stay, giving them the freedom to go where they want when they want.

There could also be fleets of taxis and shuttles that are hybrid electric/biodiesel thus having no carbon emissions. Taxis, shuttles, and buses idling and spewing CO_2 could be a thing of the past. The green taxis would be similar to any taxi on the road now, a larger sedan or maybe a sport utility wagon or an SUV painted a shade of green people could recognize.

There could be a green taxi, shuttle, and vehicle rental located near every airport. They would fuel all of the vehicles with biodiesel when they returned "home", and then send them back out once they are refueled and recharged with a 440 volt rapid re-charger system. They could be painted a shade of green so environmentally conscious passengers would recognize them. They could specialize in airport shuttle pick-up where 1-15 people going to the airport get picked up at their home of office in a hybrid shuttle van and dropped off at the airport. From the airport, another load of passengers could be picked up and each dropped off at their respective destinations such as downtown hotels, convention centers, sports venues, and other destinations.

The hybrid rental offices at every airport and anywhere else there is a car rental agency, would offer an environmentally friendly option. With a range over 1000 miles between refueling stops, most renters would use less than a tank of biodiesel. Again, they would have the option of choosing from a compact car, sedan, sports car, sport utility wagon, SUV, etc.

There could also be hybrid electric/biodiesel school and city buses that would have zero carbon emissions. They already have something similar in many cities. The buses are refueled with biodiesel and put on a 440V rapid re-charger to get them ready to go back in service. The bus station houses will have their own biodiesel pumps with giant storage tanks that do not need to be refilled as often as their current gas storage tanks. They are also less hazardous and cheaper to install.

There have been successful flights by planes running on biodiesel, but these are test flights and it may be awhile before they enter service for civilian, military, government, corporate, and other uses. There could be planes and semis running on biodiesel to meet all of the cargo transport needs as well.

New high-speed maglev trains require a new track to operate at their peak performance. That could be a great public works project, replacing all of the old track with the new high-speed tracks.

There are currently trains in Japan and China that are running from 120 mph up to 350+ mph. At these speeds, a cross country trip with limited stops could easily make it from one coast to the other in 12 to 24 hours. A person could hop on in the morning, eat breakfast, lunch, dinner, converse with other passengers in the lounge, have a drink, go back to their private room, watch cable, surf the Internet, make cell phone calls, have a snack, take a nap, and wake up when the train arrives on the opposite coast, cheaper, easier, and safer than flying.

These trains could have a special track for cargo trains that have lightweight containers made out of Kevlar and/or aluminum or some other lightweight material. These containers could be easily loaded and unloaded at each stop. This would make same day and next day deliveries pretty commonplace and much cheaper than they are today, all with zero CO_2 emissions. These containers would also be stackable and compatible with semi tractor trailers and cargo ships making them easy to load from the ship, to the train, to the truck, to the final destination.

Say No to Coal

The average American uses the electric energy equivalent of about 5 tons of coal per year. Over half of America's energy comes from coal. There are over 500 existing coal plants in 47 states, they are responsible for about 40% of US CO2 emissions. There are another 150+ proposed coal plants in the US that could very negatively affect the environment if they were to get built. There is bipartisan support among legislators for the new coal plants, but large groups of voters in many states are turning out to say no to coal.

China uses as much if not more coal than the US. China has 500+ coal plants scheduled to be built in the coming decade. This could have an extremely serious long term negative environmental impact . . .

Deforestation

Humans have been clear-cutting swaths of rainforest the size of Switzerland every year, as well as slashing and burning rainforest for cattle grazing and to grow soy, sugar, and other crops used for ethanol. Once biodiesel is being made from algae, ethanol should no longer be as important, but they could continue the deforestation of tropical rainforests for cattle grazing, fire wood, and other purposes. If reliable substitutes are not found soon, the results could be disastrous . . .

Summary

It's been said, "In an undeveloped country, do not drink the water, in a developed country do not breathe the air."[24]

Cities like Seoul, Mexico City, and even Los Angeles have occasional smog alerts and it is not uncommon to see people with surgical masks in these and many other major metropolitan areas. These new hybrids would be especially popular in these cities where gas is expensive and air pollution is a problem. Even though most of the pollution is industrial, that will all change with time too. Unfortunately, if these new hybrids became too inexpensive, populous cities would end up with a lot more traffic and congestion.

Currently, 80% of energy humans use comes from fossil fuels, 2 new coal plants are built per day. If humans could stop using fossil fuels, and stop deforestation they would be able to slow or even reverse the effects of global warming.

---

[24] *Jonathan Raban quotes.* (n.d.) retrieved from http://thinkexist.com/quotes/jonathan_raban/

Appendix D

Is the Future Foreordained?

THESE ARE A few of histories mysteries that may shed some light on the subject. If humans do not learn from history, they may be doomed to repeat it.

An interesting and uncanny historical coincidence. Both Presidents Lincoln and Kennedy were concerned with the issue of civil rights. Lincoln was elected to Congress in 1846, Kennedy was elected to Congress in 1946. Lincoln ran for the Senate in 1858, Kennedy in 1958. Lincoln was elected President in 1860; Kennedy in 1960. Both were slain on a Friday and were shot in the head. Both Lincoln and Kennedy were shot by Southerners who were known by three names. Their successors, both named Johnson, were Southern Democrats, and both were in the senate. Andrew Johnson was born in 1808 and Lyndon Johnson was born in 1908. John Wilkes Booth was born in 1839, Lee Harvey Oswald was born in 1939. Booth and Oswald were both assassinated before going to trial. Both President's wives lost children while in the White House (also interesting to note, no picture exists of Lincoln and his wife Mary together). Lincoln's secretary, named Kennedy, advised him not to go to the theater. Kennedy's secretary, whose last name was Lincoln, advised him not to go to Dallas. John Wilkes Booth shot Lincoln in a theater and ran to a warehouse. Lee Harvey Oswald shot Kennedy from a warehouse and ran to a theater. The names Lincoln and Kennedy, each contain 7 letters. The names Andrew Johnson and Lyndon Johnson each have 13 letters. The names John Wilkes Booth and Lee Harvey Oswald, each contain 15 letters.

History sometimes seems to repeat itself, there are several uncanny coincidences in history. Another uncanny coincidence involves Thomas Jefferson who wrote the Declaration of Independence and John Adams who helped edit it, the Declaration was approved by the Continental Congress on July 4, 1776, both men died 50years later to the day on July, 4, 1826.

Thomas Edison, who had a world record 1093 patents said, "If we did all of the things we are capable of doing, we could literally astound ourselves." and he proceeded to get 1093 patents for products such as the incandescent light bulb. Now the incandescent light bulb could be considered outdated and the fluorescent bulb is taking its place. What could the next generation of brilliant ideas be and where and who could they come from?

Appendix E

Endangered and Extinct Animals

African Elephant – only about 10,000 left as a result of hunting for the
    ivory trade;

African Wild Dog – numbers are down to 3000-5000 – endangered

American Alligator – Nearly extinct in 1967, they just got off of the
    endangered list

Asian Lion – 400 and counting left in the wild

Atlantic Ridley Turtle – popular as boot material and food in Mexico,
    still critical

Atlantic Salmon – several types are in decline – on the Endangered
    Species List

Bald Eagle – Once Endangered and Threatened it was de-listed in
    2007

Black Footed Ferret – brought back from extinction they continue to be
    Endangered

Black Lemur – IUCN Red List has them as vulnerable

Blue Whale – hunted to near extinction they are still an Endangered
    Species

Bowhead Whale – hunted to near extinction, populations are still
    critically endangered

California Condor – despite recovery efforts they remain critically endangered

Carolina Parakeet – **extinct** since 1918

Cheetah – fastest land animal has nowhere to run – it is considered vulnerable

Common Chimpanzee – one of our closest living relatives – endangered

Coelacanth – deep sea trawling could render them extinct (again)

Dodo – discovered in 1581 and **extinct** by 1700 due to the actions of humans

Eastern Cougar – has been on the endangered list since 1973

Eskimo Curlew – severely endangered if not extinct

Fin Whale – 2nd largest animal after the blue whale also endangered

Florida Manatee – they have rebounded from endangered to threatened and vulnerable

Galapagos Flightless Cormorant – endemic to the Galapagos, on the endangered list

Gaur – 4th largest land animal still vulnerable

Gavial – trophy hunting and used as indigenous medicine made it critically endangered

Giant Anteater – one killed a woman in 2007 – still considered vulnerable

Giant Armadillo – eats entire termite mounds – considered vulnerable

Giant Panda – less than 3000 left in the wild – rated endangered

Gorilla – closest living relative to humans after chimpanzees – endangered

Great Auk – hunted to extinction partly by humans – last seen in 1852

Greater Prairie Chicken – becoming more rare due to habitat loss – vulnerable

Green Turtle – intentionally and unintentionally killed – endangered

Grey Whale – protected since 1949 – conservation status is of least concern

Grizzly Bear – trophy hunters still a threat – conservation status – least concern

Humpback Whale – upgraded from vulnerable – still endangered in some areas

Imperial Parrot – illegal trapping & deforestation left only 150-250 – endangered

Indian Rhinoceros – about 2500 left – still considered vulnerable

Jaguar – 3rd largest feline – endangered in the US due to new border fence

Japanese Crested Ibis – brought to brink of extinction – still endangered

Kagu – hunted by humans (feathers for hats), also dogs and cats – still endangered

Kakapo – was 3rd most populous bird in New Zealand before humans – critical

Komodo Dragon – only 4000-5000 left in wild – vulnerable

Leatherback Turtle – very few survive to adulthood – critical

Leopard – smallest of the four big cats – considered near threatened

Loggerhead Turtle – fishing nets have caused many deaths – still endangered

Mediterranean Monk Seal – less than 600 – one of most endangered mammals

Monkey Eating Eagle – less than 500 in the wild – critically endangered

Mountain Gorilla – hunted and trapped for bush meat – critically endangered

Orangutan – due to human activities it has become critically endangered

Passenger Pigeon – 19th century there were billions, by the 20th cent. **extinct**

Peregrine Falcon – use of DDT endangered them, coming back gradually

Piping Plover – hunted for plumes for women's hats – near threatened

Prong horned Antelope – 5 species existed now all but one species extinct

Pygmy Hippopotamus – loss of habitat and hunting – endangered

Sea Otter – hunted to near extinction for fur – endangered

Short nose Sturgeon – over fishing, poaching – critically endangered

Snow Leopard – 3500-7000 in wild – endangered

Tapir – all 4 species considered endangered or vulnerable

Tiger – 3 of 9 species extinct – other 6 endangered – 1500-3500 in wild

Trumpeter Swan – largest native N. American bird – threatened in some areas

Vancouver Island Marmot – 220-240 in wild – critically threatened

White Pelican – conservation status – least concerned

White Rhinoceros – conservation status – near threatened

Whooping Crane – tallest N. American bird, 400 left in wild, endangered

Wild Ass – about 570 in the wild – critically endangered

Wild Yak – conservation status – vulnerable and many more are extinct or most likely could be by the end of the century. So no shark fin soup or seals balls (allegedly an aphrodisiac).

Glossary/Index

Aquaculture: also known as **aqua farming**, is the farming of aquatic Organisms such as fish, crustaceans, mollusks, and aquatic plants. Aquaculture involves cultivating freshwater and saltwater populations under controlled conditions, and can be contrasted with commercial fishing, which is the harvesting of wild fish. Aquaculture, *http:// en.wikipedia.Org/w/index.php?title=Aquaculture&oldid=412361855* (last visited Feb. 10, 2011). **page 35**

An **aquifer** is a wet underground layer of water-bearing permeable rock or consolidated materials (gravel, sand, silt, or clay) from which groundwater can be usefully extracted using a water well. Aquifer, *http://en.wikipedia.Org/w/index.php?title=Aquifer&oldid=412603783* (last visited Feb. 10, 2011). **pages 25, 27, 29**

Biodiesel: a vegetable oil or animal fat based diesel fuel that can be made from soybean oil, hemp, waste vegetable oil (WVO), animal fat, and now even algae which can grow off of sewage and does not need to take up precious farmland like most other sources. Biodiesel, *http:// en.wikipedia.Org/w/index.php?title=Biodiesel&oldid=410421633* (last visited Feb. 10, 2011). **pages 13, 28, 29, 34, 36, 40, 41, 45-49, 51, 53, 54, 56, 57, 58, 61, 62, 65, 76-86, 93**

Black Water: is waste water containing fecal matter and urine. It is also known as brown water, foul water, or sewage. It is distinct from grey water, which only contains the residues of washing processes from laundry, dishwater, and bathing. Blackwater (waste), *http://en.wikipedia. Org/w/index.php?title=Blackwater_(waste)&oldid=366892235* (last visited Feb. 10, 2011). **pages 47, 78**

Carbon Footprint: the total set of greenhouse gas (GHG) emissions caused by an Organization, event, product, or person. Carbon footprint, *http:// en.wikipedia.Org/w/index.php?title=Carbon_footprint&oldid=411146483* (last visited Feb. 10, 2011). **pages 50, 96**

Carbon Neutrality: having a net zero carbon footprint, which refers to achieving net zero carbon emissions by balancing a measured amount of carbon released with an equivalent amount sequestered or offset, or buying enough carbon credits to make up the difference. It is used in the context of carbon dioxide releasing processes, associated with transportation, energy production and industrial processes. Carbon neutrality, *http:// en.wikipedia.Org/w/index.php?title=Carbon_neutrality&oldid=411308136* (last visited Feb. 10, 2011). **pages 47, 52, 53**

Cookie Cutter Condominiums (condos): a chain of condominiums that are virtually the exact same so that production, erection, and maintenance could be cheaper than a "one of a kind" condominium, the savings can then be passed on to the consumer allowing many people that could not afford to buy real estate the chance to own their own property and build equity in it instead of paying rent. **pages 12, 14, 18, 50, 53, 54, 65, 77, 80**

Cookie Cutter Group Homes: These could be mass produced, easy to erect, easy to maintain structures that could house any number of people and would be cheaper than building "one of a kind" homes. Residents typically have their own sleeping room and share a bathroom and possibly a kitchen and a laundry room on each floor. There could also be a cafeteria or food court on one level and lots of other amenities delivered to the end consumer at a much lower cost than their "one of a kind" counterparts. **pages 50, 51, 86, 89**

Cookie Cutter Retirement Villas: These could be villas of any size where every building, inside and out, is mass produced making them cheaper to build, erect, and maintain than "one of a kind" villas. They would most likely be for the cost conscious retirees and offer lots of amenities for a fraction of the cost of a similar "one of a kind" villas elsewhere. **pages 13, 55, 56, 66, 80, 84**

Deforestation is the removal of a forest or stand of trees where the land is thereafter converted to a non forest use. Examples of deforestation include conversion of forestland to agriculture or urban use. It has been estimated that about half of the Earth's mature tropical forests have now been cleared. Some scientists have predicted that unless significant measures (such as seeking out and protecting old growth forests that have not been disturbed) are taken on a worldwide basis, by 2030 there could only be ten percent remaining, with another ten percent in a degraded condition. 80% could have been lost, and with them hundreds of thousands of irreplaceable species. Estimates vary widely as to the extent of tropical deforestation. *Scientists estimate* that one fifth of the world's tropical rainforest was destroyed between 1960 and 1990. They claim that that rainforests 50 years ago covered 14% of the world's land surface, now only cover 5-7%, and *that all tropical forests could be gone by the middle of the 21st century.* Deforestation, *http://en.wikipedia.Org/w/ index.php?title=Deforestation&oldid=413026556* (last visited Feb. 10, 2011). **pages 35, 73, 75, 80, 87, 91**

Desalination (Desal) Plant: Also referred to as a desalinization plant. Water is desalinated in order to convert salt water to fresh water so it is suitable for human consumption or irrigation. Sometime the process produces table salt as a by product. Desalination, *http://en.wikipedia. Org/w/index.php?title=Desalination&oldid=412964159* (last visited Feb. 10, 2011). **pages 13, 25-29, 33, 36, 38, 62, 63, 76, 78, 79–also Page 97–**

Desertification: is the degradation of land in arid and dry sub-humid areas due to various factors including climactic variations and human activities Desertification, *http://en.wikipedia.Org/w/index.php?title=Dese rtification&oldid=412165965* (last visited Feb. 10, 2011). **pages 25-29, 73, 74, 78, 80**

Ecotourism: This is responsible travel to fragile, pristine, and usually protected areas that strive to be low impact and often a small scale alternative to mass tourism. Its purpose is to educate the traveler; provide funds for ecological conservation; directly benefit the economic development and political empowerment of local communities; and foster respect for different cultures and for human rights. Ecotourism, *http://en.wikipedia.Org/w/index.php?title=Ecotourism&oldid=412778592* (last visited Feb. 10, 2011). **page 56**

Fast Track Guidance Program – This could be a computer program and database that gives every individual a battery of tests (such as intelligence and aptitude) and records and compares all of their results and tracks their ongoing progress. The results are discussed with each individual by a licensed guidance counselor until they have completed their education and are placed in the perfect position for them. **pages 12, 65, 68, 69, 78, 79**

Fossil Fuel: The fossil fuels, which contain high percentages of carbon, include coal, petroleum, and natural gas. Fossil fuel, *http://en.wikipedia. Org/w/index.php?title=Fossil_fuel&oldid=411232135* (last visited Feb. 10, 2011). **pages 81, 82, 84, 87**

Global Village: This is usually used as a metaphor to describe the Internet and World Wide Web. On the Internet, physical distance is even less of a hindrance to the real time communicative activities of people, and therefore social spheres are greatly expanded by the openness of the web and the ease at which people can search for online communities and interact with others that share the same interests and concerns. Therefore, this technology fosters the idea of a conglomerate yet unified global community. Global village (term), *http://en.wikipedia.Org/w/ index.php?title=Global_village_(term)&oldid=404396309* (last visited Feb. 10, 2011). **page 24**

Global warming is the increase in the average temperature of Earth's near-surface air and oceans since the mid-20th century and its projected continuation. According to the 2007 Fourth Assessment report by the Intergovernmental Panel on Climate Change (IPCC), global surface temperature increased 0.74 +/- 0.18 degrees Celsius during the 20th century. Most of the observed temperature increase since the middle of the 20th century has been caused by increasing concentrations of greenhouse gases, which result from human activity such as the burning of fossil fuel and deforestation. Global warming, *http://en.wikipedia. Org/w/index.php?title=Global_warming&oldid=412800655* (last visited Feb. 10, 2011). **page 87**

Grey water recycling: Grey water is wastewater generated from domestic activities such as laundry, dishwashing, and bathing, which can be recycled on-site for uses such as landscape irrigation and constructed wetlands. It can also be used to flush toilets (black water contains human waste) in homes and buildings where it is treated on-site and piped back into the toilet. Grey water composes 50-80% of residential wastewater generated from all of the house's sanitation equipment (except toilets). Greywater, *http://en.wikipedia.Org/w/index.php?title=Greywater&oldid= 412425853* (last visited Feb. 10, 2011). **pages 37, 47, 50, 55, 78**

Groundwater is water located beneath the ground surface in soil pore spaces and in the fractures of rock formations. A unit of rock or an unconsolidated deposit is called an aquifer when it can yield a usable quantity of water. The depth at which soil pore spaces or fractures and voids in rock become completely saturated with water is called the water table. Groundwater is recharged from, and eventually flows to, the surface naturally; natural discharge often occurs at springs and seeps, and can form oases or wetlands. Groundwater is also often withdrawn for agricultural, municipal, and industrial use by constructing and operating extraction wells. Groundwater, *http://en.wikipedia.Org/w/index.php?title=Groundwa ter&oldid=413098637* (last visited Feb. 10, 2011). **pages 25, 26**

High-Speed Rail: In the US, high-speed rail is defined as having a speed above 100 mph (180km/h). In Japan, some high-speed trains travel in excess of 160 mph (260 km/h). In China, there are two grades of high-speed lines: slower lines running at 120 and 160 mph (200 and 250 km/h) which may comprise either freight or passenger trains. Secondly, passenger dedicated lines operate at top speeds of up to 220 mph (350 km/h). High-speed rail, *http://en.wikipedia.Org/w/index. php?title=High-speed_rail&oldid=412930694* (last visited Feb. 10, 2011). **pages 13, 36, 53, 54, 77, 86**

Hydroponics: This is a method of growing plants using mineral nutrient solutions, in water, without soil. Terrestrial plants may be grown with their roots in the mineral solution only or an inert medium, such as perlite, gravel, mineral wool, or coconut husk. Hydroponics, *http:// en.wikipedia.Org/w/index.php?title=Hydroponics&oldid=413120795* (last visited Feb. 10, 2011). **pages 38, 54**

Humanure: is human excrement (feces and urine) that is recycled via composting for agricultural or other purposes. Humanure, *http:// en.wikipedia.Org/w/index.php?title=Humanure&oldid=388323151* (last visited Feb. 10, 2011). **pages 37, 38, 47, 78, 80**

International Service: This could be the international equivalent of National Service. When students complete their studies at the World Class Academy near them, they would then sign up for a two or more year commitment to do some sort of International Service, such as being a UN Peacekeeper. **pages 57, 69, 70**

Maglev high-speed Trains: This method has the potential to be faster, quieter, and smoother than wheeled mass transit systems. Maglev (transport), *http://en.wikipedia.Org/w/index.php?title=Maglev_ (transport)&oldid=418301468* (last visited Mar. 12, 2011). **pages 13, 36, 53, 54, 77, 86**

Mass Production: This term was first used around 1926 and means the production of large amounts of standardized products such as household appliances and automobiles. Mass production, *http://en.wikipedia.Org/w/ index.php?title=Mass_production&oldid=412959789* (last visited Feb. 10, 2011). **pages 26, 27, 33, 34, 35, 38, 44-47, 49-53, 56, 57, 67, 70, 77, 78**

Match Maker Program: This could be the next generation of the current dating sites. Its goal could be to help every individual find their life mate, especially for purposes of breeding children. **pages 12, 20, 55, 65, 78, 79**

Multinational Corporations: A corporation or an enterprise that manages production or delivers services in more than one country. Multinational corporation, *http://en.wikipedia.Org/w/index. php?title=Multinational_corporation&oldid=411452800* (last visited Feb. 10, 2011). **page 74**

National Academy: This could be an academy for students aged 13-18 where they would live on-site and have more courses and extracurricular activities than an average school could possibly offer. It could also be a preparatory academy for National Service. One goal could be to create a truly integrated learning environment where students from every possible subgroup could come together and live, study, work, and play as one group. **pages 12, 13, 49, 51, 55, 65-69, 70, 79**

National Service: This could be an optional or mandatory term of service in either a branch of the military; a government agency; the Peace Corps, Americorps-Vista; or missionary work for a church, charity, or Nonprofit Organization. The possibilities are endless. **pages 12, 13, 18, 24, 55, 57, 64, 65, 68, 69, 70, 76, 79**

New Mobile Home Park: These could be in the city, suburbs, or more likely in rural areas and would have new advanced mobile homes on lots that can be purchased. They could have several amenities such as an indoor/outdoor pool, all within the community. **pages 48, 49, 50, 65, 77, 80**

Noblesse Oblige is generally used to imply that with wealth, power and prestige come responsibilities. The phrase is sometimes used derisively, in the sense of condescending or hypocritical social responsibility. In American English especially, the term has also been applied more broadly to those who are capable of simple acts to help another, usually one who is less fortunate. Noblesse oblige, *http://en.wikipedia.Org/w/ index.php?title=Noblesse_oblige&oldid=411527816* (last visited Feb. 10, 2011). **pages 13, 19, 42, 68**

Oil Independence: This could be part of a Fossil Fuel Free by 2030 campaign that would attempt to find replacements for all fossil fuels by the year 2030. Sweden has a similar program that aims to have the nation fossil fuel free by 2020. Making Sweden an Oil-Free Society, *http://en.wikipedia.Org/w/index.php?title=Making_Sweden_an_Oil-Free_ Society&oldid=400903047* (last visited Feb. 10, 2011). **page 84**

Overfishing: This occurs when fishing activities reduce fish stocks below an acceptable level. This can occur in any body of water. An example would be the Atlantic Cod which was so over fished in the 1970's and 80's it led to a sharp decrease in the number of Atlantic Cod. Over-fishing can also ultimately upset entire marine ecosystems such as the over fishing of sharks is potentially going to do. Overfishing, *http:// en.wikipedia.Org/w/index.php?title=Overfishing&oldid=408275414* (last visited Feb. 10, 2011). **pages 35, 74, 92**

Overpopulation: The world's population has significantly increased in the last 50 years, mainly due to medical advancements and substantial increases in agricultural productivity. The recent rapid rise in human population over the past two centuries has raised concerns that humans are beginning to overpopulate the earth., and that this planet may no be able to sustain present or larger numbers of inhabitants. The population has been growing continuously since the end of the Black Death around the year 1400; at the beginning of the 19th century, it had reached roughly 1 billion. Increases in life expectancy and resource availability during the industrial and green revolutions led to rapid growth on a worldwide level. By 1960, the world population had reached 3 billion; it doubled to 6 billion by 2000. The population is expected to reach 8 billion by 2040 and 10.5 billion by 2050. Overpopulation, *http://en.wikipedia.Org/w/index.php?title=Overpopulation&oldid=413016596* (last visited Feb. 10, 2011). **pages 19, 57**

Papercrete: This is a recently developed construction material which consists of re-pulped paper fiber with Portland cement or clay and/or other soil added. Papercrete, *http://en.wikipedia.Org/w/index.php?title=Papercrete&oldid=411338352* (last visited Feb. 10, 2011). **pages 47, 52**

Parenting Classes/Licensing/Insurance/Standards: These could be optional or mandatory for anyone preparing to raise a child (female and male). The classes could prepare them mentally, physically, and financially for the onus of parenting. They would then take a final exam and obtain a parenting license. Prospective parents could also be required to obtain insurance and meet a parenting standard every year. **pages 9, 12, 13, 15, 18-23, 41, 45, 58, 59, 65, 76, 79**

Peak Natural Gas: This is the point in time at which the maximum global natural gas production rate is reached, after which the rate of production enters its terminal decline. If usage stays the same, experts say there should be about 60 years worth left on earth. Peak gas, *http://en.wikipedia.Org/w/index.php?title=Peak_gas&oldid=395926767* (last visited Feb. 10, 2011). **pages 54, 74, 77, 82, 84**

Peak Oil: This is the point in time when the maximum rate of global petroleum extraction is reached, after which the rate of production enters terminal decline. Most professional estimates say that we may have reached peak oil or could reach it shortly. Peak oil, *http://en.wikipedia.*

Org/w/index.php?title=Peak_oil&oldid=412995872 (last visited Feb. 10, 2011). **pages 36, 37, 74, 84**

Peak Phosphorous: Phosphorus supplies are essential to farming and depletion of reserves is estimated at somewhere from 60 to 130 years . . . without a recycling initiative America's supply is estimated around 30 years. Hubbert peak theory, *http://en.wikipedia.Org/w/index.php?title=Hubbert_ peak_theory&oldid=412420469* (last visited Feb. 10, 2011). **pages 37, 74** (http:// en.wikipedia.Org/wiki/Peak_phosphorus#Phosphorus)

Peak Soil: Soil erosion is fast becoming one of the worlds greatest problems. The phenomenon is being called Peak Soil because large scale factory farming techniques are jeopardizing humanity's ability to grow food in the present and in the future. Without efforts to improve soil management practices, the availability of arable soil could become increasingly problematic. Some soil management techniques that may help save the soil are 1) no till farming; 2) keyline design 3) windbreaks; 4) incorporating Organic matter; and 5) stop using chemical fertilizers (which contain salt).Sustainable agriculture, *http://en.wikipedia.Org/w/ index.php?title=Sustainable_agriculture&oldid=412577139* (last visited Feb. 10, 2011). **pages 35-37, 74** (http://en.wikipedia.Org/wiki/ Sustainable_agriculture#Soil)

Photovoltaics (PV) is a method of generating electrical power by converting solar radiation into direct current electricity using semi-conductors that exhibit the photovoltaic effect. Photovoltaic power generation employs solar panels comprising of a number of cells containing a photovoltaic material. Photovoltaics, *http://en.wikipedia. Org/w/index.php?title=Photovoltaics&oldid=413122288* (last visited Feb. 10, 2011). **pages 47, 49, 52, 53**

Preventive medicine: This refers to measures taken to prevent diseases, or injuries rather than curing them or treating their symptoms. Preventive medicine, *http://en.wikipedia.Org/w/index.php?title=Preventive_ medicine&oldid=413116567* (last visited Feb. 10, 2011). **pages 40, 67**

Resomation: This is a specific alkaline hydrolysis process for the disposal of human remains, which is claimed by its creators to be much more ecologically favorable than cremation. In resomation the body is placed in a silk bag, itself placed within a metal cage frame. This is then loaded into a Resomator. The machine is filled with a mixture of water and potassium hydroxide, and heated to a high temperature (around 160 degrees Celsius), but at a high pressure, which prevents boiling. Instead, the body is effectively dissolved into its chemical components and ash, which takes about 3 hours. The end result is a small quantity of green-brown tinted liquid (containing amino acids, peptides, sugars, and salts) and soft porous white bone remains easily crushed in the hand. The white ash can be returned to the next of kin and the liquid recycled back into the ecosystem such as a memorial garden or forest. it is currently being practiced in Minnesota. Resomation, *http://en.wikipedia.Org/w/index.php?title=Resomation&oldid= 412886594* (last visited Feb. 10, 2011). **pages 37, 55, 59, 78, 80**

Self Contained Cities: These could be any size and house any number of people. They could also be mass produced and have the option of adding to them as population grows. They could all have the same amenities such as an international food court, indoor/outdoor pool with water slides "for the kids" + hot tubs for the adults. There could also be daycare/kindergarten/grade school academy on-site. They would be similar to a mixed use residential property with restaurants and shops on the ground floor accessible from inside or outside + sidewalk cafes, etc. **pages 52-54**

Solar Energy: There are two types of solar energy; active would be like photovoltaic panels that turn sunlight into electricity; and passive solar which might be a solarium or sunroom on the south side of a home. Solar energy, *http://en.wikipedia.Org/w/index.php?title=Solar_ energy&oldid=411102532* (last visited Feb. 10, 2011). **pages 28, 29, 33, 36, 38, 47, 49, 52-55, 57, 59, 77, 83**

Solar Hot Water: There are two types of solar hot water (SHW) passive and active. Both use the sun to heat water for use in homes or buildings. Solar water heating, *http://en.wikipedia.Org/w/index.php?title=Solar_ water_heating&oldid=412553530* (last visited Feb. 10, 2011). **pages 52, 54, 58, 59, 60, 86**

Sustainability: is the capacity to endure. In ecology, the word describes how biological systems remain diverse and productive over time. Long-lived and healthy wetlands and forests are examples of sustainable biological systems. For humans, sustainability is the potential for long-term maintenance of well being, which has environmental, economic, and social dimensions. Sustainability, *http://en.wikipedia. Org/w/index.php?title=Sustainability&oldid=413027367* (last visited Feb. 10, 2011). **page 36**

Sustainable agriculture: is the practice of farming using principles of ecology, the study of relationships between Organism and their environment. It has been defined as "an integrated system of plant and animal production practices having a site-specific application that could last over the long term: and: satisfy human food and fiber needs; make the most efficient use of non-renewable resources and on-farm resources and integrate, where appropriate, natural biological cycles and controls; sustain the economic viability of farm operations; enhance the quality of life for farmers and society as a whole." Sustainable agriculture, *http://en.wikipedia.Org/w/index.php?title=Sustainable_ agriculture&oldid=412577139* (last visited Feb. 10, 2011). **page 40**

Thermal Expansion: is the tendency of matter to change in volume in response to a change in temperature. All materials have this tendency. Thermal expansion, *http://en.wikipedia.Org/w/index.php?title=Thermal_ expansion&oldid=412535023* (last visited Feb. 10, 2011). **page 26**

Urban Sprawl: also known as **suburban** sprawl, is a multifaceted concept, which includes the spreading outwards of a city and its suburbs to its outskirts to low-density and auto-dependent development on rural land, high segregation of uses (e.g. stores and residential), and various design features that encourage car dependency. (^ *What is Sprawl?. SprawlCity.Org.* Retrieved on 2008-02-07.) As a result, many urban planners, government officials, and social scientist contend that sprawl has a number of disadvantages, including: high car dependence; inadequate facilities, e.g.: cultural, emergency, health, etc.; low public support for sprawl; high per-person infrastructure costs; inefficient street layouts; inflated costs for public transportation; lost time and productivity for commuting; high levels of racial and socioeconomic segregation; low diversity of housing and business types; high rates of obesity due to less walking and biking; less space for conservation and parks; high per-capita use of energy, land, and water; and perceived low aesthetic value. Urban sprawl, *http://en.wikipedia.Org/w/index.php?title=Urban_ sprawl&oldid=413012202* (last visited Feb. 10, 2011). **page 53, 77**

Vertical Farming: is a theoretical form of agriculture involving large-scale urban farming in skyscrapers. The concept was first developed in 1999 at Columbia University by American ecologist Dickson Despommier. Using advanced greenhouse technology such as hydroponics and aeroponics, these "farm scrapers" could theoretically produce fish, poultry, fruit, and vegetables. Vertical farming, *http://en.wikipedia.Org/w/ index.php?title=Vertical_farming&oldid=410964544* (last visited Feb. 10, 2011). **page 38, 54**

Water Displacement Theory: This could be mass producing water desalination plants and strategically placing them up and down the coasts of every continent, then using a series of pipelines, manmade canals, irrigation ditches, etc. to get water to every person and farm on earth. Every arable acre would be irrigated and every human being would have access to an abundance of water for drinking, bathing, cleaning, and more. One pipeline could be irrigation water, a separate pipeline could carry potable water possibly fortified with such things as vitamins and minerals, and with other additives such as fluoride and iodine. This would prevent any child from ever dying from dehydration again, and it would reverse the effects of rising sea levels and desertification by draining 250+million gallons of water per day times 1000's of desal plants worldwide. It could also produce a whole lotta table salt. **page 26**

Wind Power: is the conversion of wind energy into a useful form of energy, such as using wind turbines to make electricity, wind mills for mechanical power, wind pumps for pumping water or drainage, or sails to propel ships. Wind power, *http://en.wikipedia.Org/w/index.php?title=Wind_ power&oldid=412704186* (last visited Feb. 10, 2011). **pages 28, 29, 36, 38, 47, 53-55, 59, 77, 83-85**

World Class International Academy: This could be an internationally franchised academy where students of every age could study. It could be modeled on some of the better and more effective academies in existence. There may be students living on-site. There could be college preparatory courses that would prepare the students to study at any University in the world. One goal would be to get every person in the world to know English as their primary or secondary language. **pages 68, 70**

www.ingramcontent.com/pod-product-compliance
Lightning Source LLC
Chambersburg PA
CBHW070204290526
45789CB00002B/908